Drugs and the Party Line

drugs
and the party line

kevin williamson
FOREWORD BY IRVINE WELSH

This edition first published in Great Britain in 1997
by Rebel Inc., an imprint of Canongate Books Ltd,
14 High Street, Edinburgh EH1 1TE

Copyright © Kevin Williamson, 1997
Foreword copyright © Irvine Welsh, 1997

British Library Cataloguing-in-Publication Data

A catalogue record for this volume is available
on request from the British Library

ISBN 0 86241 647 7

Typeset by Palimpsest Book Production Limited,
Polmont, Stirlingshire
Printed and bound by Caledonian
Book Manufacturing, Bishopbriggs, Scotland

CONTENTS

For Keith Hellawell

"That humanity at large will ever be able to dispense with artificial paradises seems very unlikely. Most men and women lead lives at the worst so painful, at the best so monotonous, poor and limited, that the urge to escape, the longing to transcend themselves if only for a few moments, is and always has been one of the principal appetites of the soul."

ALDOUS HUXLEY,
THE DOORS OF PERCEPTION, 1951

"In my study of drugs I have been forced to run grave risks, and I have been stymied constantly by the barbarous laws under which their usage is controlled. These crude laws and the social hysteria of which they are a symptom have from day to day placed me at the edge of the gallows leap. I demand that these laws be changed."

ALEXANDER TROCCHI,
CAIN'S BOOK, 1961

FOREWORD

We live in a drug society, a chemical society. This is not new, it's always been the case that throughout recorded history people have ingested substances in order to achieve either an altered state of consciousness or simply some form of arousal or relaxation. What has happened recently concerning drugs is much the same as has happened in all other walks of life within our consumer capitalist society: there has been an expansion in the number of products available to the customer.

The notion of a society in which altered states of conscious-ness or arousal are legitimately achieved through ingesting a substance is implicitly backed by drug companies which are licensed (ie: sponsored by the state). These companies are in the business of promoting and creating products to compete with non-licensed drugs. If you think this is fanciful, look at the way Coca-Cola is advertised. A fizzy drink which has caffeine as its active ingredient is advertised as if it had the properties of MDMA, LSD or cocaine. Alcopops like Hooch, which aim to get youngsters using the drug alcohol as early as possible, have been given an "acid house" image in terms of marketing and packaging.

There is probably too much profit involved to change things now. Brewers, distillers, pubs, and off-licences will never stop selling drugs for profit as long as there's a market. Similarly, private individuals will never stop selling drugs for profit as long as there's a market. And there is: the demand for all drugs almost always exceeds the supply.

The state has an ambivalent relationship with drugs. The Conservative Party relies on (legal) drugs barons to donate money to its coffers and rewards them with knighthoods and seats on Government bodies. The Labour Party would probably take the same line if drugs companies were to offer them sponsorship.

Other drugs dealers are thrown into prison and given heavy sentences from the authorities, even for the sale of non-dangerous drugs like cannabis, which accounts for nearly 80% of drugs convictions in Britain.

All political parties find it expedient to (selectively) condemn drugs. Drug dealers are portrayed as a cause, rather than an effect, of the type of society we live in. In Scotland a body called *Scotland Against Drugs* was set up by Michael Forsyth (then Scottish Secretary whose constituency included Dunblane but whose Government would not ban handguns), George Robertson (then Labour shadow secretary), Jim Wallace (Liberal Democrats) and Alex Salmond (SNP) and the Chairman of Kwik-Fit UK, Tom Farmer. They were photographed around some clubs looking uncomfortable in sweatshirts and baseball caps. As some wag in the Basement Bar in Edinburgh said: "five sweatshirts in search of a suit." Of course, this patronising nonsense fooled nobody. The logic, as Spock from Star Trek might have said, was inescapable:

SCOTLAND AGAINST DRUGS IS **NOT** AGAINST DRUGS.

(1) ALCOHOL AND TOBACCO ARE DRUGS

(2) SCOTLAND AGAINST DRUGS ARE **NOT** AGAINST ALCOHOL AND TOBACCO

SCOTLAND AGAINST DRUGS IS **NOT** AGAINST DRUGS

SCOTLAND AGAINST DRUGS CLAIM TO BE AGAINST WHAT THEY
ARE MANIFESTLY NOT AGAINST.

Such people we normally refer to as "hypocrites", or, if they're
running for office, "politicians".

The politicians are the legislators and the legal status of a drug
is to do with historical, social, political and economic issues, it has
nothing to do with the toxicity or addictive qualities of that drug, or
the social harm that drug might do. Nobody with any intelligence
at all could deny that our drug laws are a mess, basically aimed
at protecting the market for corporate pushers who show their
gratitude with donations.

Labour's George Robertson, in myth perpetuating nonsense,
recently advocated special penalties for dealers who ply their evil
trade close to schools. Commander John Grieve, former head of
Criminal Intelligence at the Metropolitan Police, who might be
expected to know a bit more about this issue than Robertson (as
might just about anybody, with the possible exception of Michael
Forsyth) said: "*You are more likely to be offered drugs for the first
time by a member of your family or a close friend than by the
archetypal stranger at the school gates. When parents demand we
arrest the dealers, it is their own children they are referring to.*"

I look forward to a Labour Government shutting down all
the pubs and off-licences within a designated distance of each
Scottish school's gates. When that happens, we really will be
making serious inroads into the "drugs problem". Don't hold
your breath. In the meantime somebody ought to tell George
Robertson that thinking on your feet and talking through your
arse are not the same thing.

We have to remember that preachers generally preach to meet
their own needs, not anyone else's. Phony drugs wars are seldom,
in reality, targeted at the people who are actually taking drugs.

They are invariably just a sad attempt to con frightened people who will never take drugs into believing that something is being done, when the very reverse is true. People are dying because *nothing* at all is being done, and anti-drugs propaganda merely reinforces an unworkable and dangerous status quo.

There can be little doubt that increasing levels of social inequality and poverty and a decreasing of employment opportunities will lead to an increase in the misuse of opiates, alcohol and other downers, as people seek temporary respite from social pressure. The phrase "getting out of it" springs to mind. Surely if "it" was better, then so many people wouldn't need to get out of it so often.

In this book Kevin Williamson has tried to sweep aside some of the bullshit in order to make sense of an issue which is shrouded in lies, disinformation and hysteria. He also presents a set of practical suggestions, which, whether one agrees or disagrees with them, offer a consistent alternative to the current mess and open up the whole issue for real discussion and debate.

And we need to do that before we can do anything else.

Irvine Welsh

AN INTRODUCTION

When it comes to drug use we live in a climate of fear. Those who don't take illicit drugs are afraid of those who do, and those who do take them are afraid of being caught. And all the time, the flames of fear are fanned by a media which is often ill-informed and at times both hysterical and hypocritical.

It is little wonder that few drug users will raise their heads over the parapet to speak out on the subject. To admit to taking illegal drugs is to risk losing your job, being denied entry to certain countries, and to risk being ostracised from elements within your community or even close family. This makes the debate on drugs very one-sided.

Politically it is even worse. Anyone who suggests that the current drug laws and drug policies should be reviewed or changed is immediately slammed as being pro-drug. It is easier to bang the law-and-order drum than address complex social questions. So most politicians either stay silent or join in the knee-jerk anti-drugs crusades that crop up with depressing regularity. And nothing changes.

This book was initially conceived as a reaction to the way that a few well-publicised drug-related deaths were used by certain individuals in the media to orchestrate what amounted to a yet another witchhunt against those people who use illicit drugs. Drugs are depicted as an evil in our midst, drug dealers as a menace that have to be stamped out, and drug users are being portrayed as sad, pathetic victims.

But this flies in the face of what I have seen with my own eyes. Most people I know who use illicit drugs are just normal folk getting on with their lives, people having a bit of fun at the weekend, or individuals who smoke the occasional joint to relax or unwind with friends. In the main, most drug users aren't addicts nor do they have a problem with drugs. Yet they are treated like criminals.

There is always some Chief Constable who wants to make a name for himself. A clampdown on drug users is an easy option. Send in the riot squad, turn over a few pre-club bars, and round up the usual suspects. It's open season on drug users.

Questions need to be asked in order to try and make sense of what's going on. Questions which challenge the accepted wisdom on the subject. Questions like: Why are some drugs prohibited while the sale of others are licensed? Does drug prohibition actually work or does it make the situation worse? Do high-profile anti-drug campaigns make any difference?

It is these three questions that form the basis of the first section of the book. As well as looking at drug prohibition in general, and the on-going War Against Drugs, I've given the *Scotland Against Drugs* campaign lengthy and detailed analysis because it is supported by all the major political parties in the UK and is indicative of their current thinking. As is so often the case, Scotland is used as a political testing ground for controversial ideas. However this time, unlike with the hated poll tax a few years back, hopefully enough people will see the mistakes made by the *SAD* campaign to avoid repetition in the rest of the country.

The conclusion that these chapters come to is that *drug prohibition* and *high-profile anti-drug campaigns* are *directly* responsible for *most of the problems* associated with illegal drugs rather than being part of the solution. I would challenge anyone who supports the current drug laws to put their hand on their heart and say with conviction that the current drug policies are working. And then provide evidence to prove it. Here is the evidence which says they aren't.

The latter section of this book then goes on to put forward the case for a new and radical approach which – if politicians have the courage to implement – will benefit both drug users and the wider community as a whole. If acted upon, hard evidence suggests that:

- Property crimes such as car-theft and housebreaking will plummet.
- New cases of drug addiction will fall dramatically.
- Overall drug use will drop.
- Organised crime will suffer a major blow.
- The damage that drugs do to people's health will be substantially reduced.
- Police and courts will have time freed up to deal with serious crime.
- 6–7 million people in the UK will no longer be criminalised for using drugs.[1]
- The climate of fear that surrounds drug use will be lifted.

Whether these are wild and fantastical claims or are based on policies of common sense, unavoidable evidence, and the results of experiments in drug policy that have already taken place, readers will have to judge for themselves.

While this book considers that drug use means all drugs, legal and illegal, it has in the main stuck to the problems associated with currently prohibited substances. A separate section dealing with such legal drugs as alcohol, tobacco, prescribed drugs, tranquillisers, and solvents may be included in a future edition.

But the purpose of this edition is to try and raise questions about the current drug laws, attitudes, and methods of drug education. And to put up for discussion concrete proposals for change.

Nobody could really claim to have all the answers to such a diverse and complex issue as drug use but anyone who looks objectively at the current situation would have to admit that it is the worst of all possible worlds.

And finally, this is not a pro-drugs book. The decision to take drugs should be a personal one and it isn't the place of myself or anyone else to encourage or advocate drug use. That goes as much for legal drugs as illegal ones.

DRUG PROHIBITION: HOW IT CAME ABOUT

"Stringent laws, spectacular police drives, vigorous prosecution and imprisonment of addicts and peddlers have proved not only useless and enormously expensive as means of correcting this evil, but they are also unjustifiably and unbelievably cruel in their application to the unfortunate drug victims."

AUGUST VOLLMER, 1936[1]
Chief of Police in Berkeley, California
and former President of the International Association of Chiefs of Police

History is that most contentious of subjects as it is the one subject that always puts into perspective the temporary nature of all laws, ideas, morals, attitudes, and even economic systems. An honest study of history will always prove that nothing lasts forever and nowhere more so than in the field of human affairs. This includes the current drug laws as much as anything else.

Throughout history there have been all sorts of attempts to prohibit or regulate the use of certain drugs. But there are few explanations of *why* this is done. It is generally assumed – and rarely questioned – that it is all done for the greatest possible good. Drug taking causes health and social problems and the prohibitionists want to help sort out these problems because of their love for their fellow man. In other words the roots of prohibition are portrayed as humanitarian.

However, a closer look at the origins of prohibition exposes this as one of the great deceptions in the whole drug debate and one that needs challenging. Behind the cloak of humanitarianism lurks vested interests – both economic and ideological.

EARLY ATTEMPTS AT PROHIBITION

When the prophet Mohammed (?570-632AD) decided to outlaw the use of alcohol among his followers, it was probably the first large scale attempt at drug prohibition in history. The banning of alcohol was done to differentiate the followers of Mohammed from the early Christians who had adopted alcohol as the official drug of their religion. The early Christians had elevated the use of alcohol in accordance with the example set by their leader, Jesus, whose first miracle, they believed, was to turn water into wine, and whose final act at the Last Supper was to sanctify wine as a holy sacrament (the blood of Christ).

Although Mohammed didn't know it at the time, a pattern was being established, that would continue. The banning of alcohol was for ideological reasons alone. Alcohol was the drug of the religious competition and by forbidding it Mohammed was creating a unifying factor among his people. This policy of alcohol prohibition still holds firm in many Islamic countries today.

The use of drug prohibition as a tool of social control would continue down the years. As explorers and Christian missionaries ventured abroad they discovered strange new lands which were home to people with exotic customs and rituals involving plant drugs such as peyote, coca, tobacco and hallucinogenic fungi. At first, they thought these indigenous peoples were possessed by "the devil" as they went into unexplainable drug-induced trances. Later they would subject these native cultures to a crude bludgeoning and without exception the drugs used by these cultures were prohibited and driven underground by the European invaders. In some instances – such as with the advanced Inca and Aztec civilisations of central America whose people worshipped the coca and peyote plant gods – an entire culture was extinguished in what would now be termed mass genocide. The purpose of these bloodthirsty attacks by the European invaders on peaceful societies was recorded at the time as a spiritual crusade against heresy (the Inquisition was still alive and kicking) but it soon became apparent that it was in fact the plunder of gold, mineral reserves, and land that were the real objectives. The conquerors understood that in order to plunder these riches the native cultures first had to be crushed or made subservient to the new rulers. This meant banning the drugs and pagan rituals which played a central role in their religions and social organisation. Thus drug prohibition was used as the cutting edge of social control.

When you look around the world now, at the end of the twentieth century, and see what the banning of these paganistic religions and their ritual plant drugs has done (and their enforced replacement by Christianity and alcohol) for native Americans, Fijians, Aborigines, Maoris and many others, it could hardly be considered as a humanitarian gesture.

TOBACCO

The first serious attempt at drug prohibition in the British Isles followed the discovery of tobacco in 1585 by Sir Walter Raleigh. After its introduction to Britain, tobacco "drinking", as it was often called, became all the fashion among the aristocracy and noblemen. In his book *The Faerie Queene*, Edmund Spenser described it as "divine tobacco." Immediately, just like the later discoveries of such drugs as cocaine, heroin and amphetamine, it was hailed as a new wonder medicine. It was claimed to be effective against fevers, headaches, chilblains and even venereal disease.[2] Tobacco only seemed to have one drawback – it created a powerful craving after it had been used for a period of time.

The backlash against tobacco duly followed. England was in the grip of Puritanism. The immediate "divine" pleasures of tobacco and the relaxed sociable way it was taken were alien to the piety and work ethic of the new religion. The first pamphlet denouncing recreational use of tobacco, *Work for Chimney Sweeps*, was written in 1602 by Philaretes who denounced it as "a pestiferous vice." This preceded a more famous work published two years later, *Counterblast to Tobacco*, written by the newly ascended monarch to the throne, King James I.

King James denounced tobacco as "a stinking loathsome thing" which was "the lively image and pattern of hell." But he decided that an outright ban on tobacco was unfeasible. To outlaw the now-favoured drug of many royal courtiers may have instigated rebellion in their midst. These were troubled political times when monarchs and aristocrats could lose their heads if they weren't careful.

King James chose a different approach to deal with the escalation in tobacco use. He imposed a 4,000 per cent increase on its custom duty[3], thereby hoping to reduce its consumption among the commoners – who were now taking to the new drug in great numbers – while leaving it as a preserve of the rich. It was a form of indirect prohibition.

King James understood that the working men who used tobacco were taking time off work to smoke. James also understood that when working men came together in huddled groups to smoke the talk could quickly turn to gunpowder and treason.

But just as later exponents of drug prohibition were to discover, the imposition of such a heavy tax merely succeeded in driving the import of tobacco into the hands of smugglers. By 1608 King James' hostility to tobacco had been overtaken by economic considerations. He needed the money. So he worked out a level of customs duty which was low enough to deter the retailers from finding it more profitable to buy their supplies from the black market.

Then, in another reversal of policy, in 1620 the British colony of Virginia was encouraged to grow tobacco for domestic British consumption. Parliament of that year calculated that this would generate a six-figure sum which otherwise would have gone to Britain's colonial rivals via the Portuguese and Spanish colonies in the Americas.[4]

In sixteen short years tobacco had gone from being denounced as "an evil" to the stage where its cultivation and import were enthusiastically encouraged for economic reasons. Humanitarian concern for the health of the common people never even entered the King's calculations.

ALCOHOL

The next targeted drug of modern-day prohibitionists was alcohol. In the nineteenth century a campaign got underway to have alcohol classified as a dangerous drug and to have it banned from general consumption. In a forerunner of the so-called 'gateway drug theory' or the 'slippery slope theory' some of the alcohol prohibitionists believed that the most effective way to reduce the use of alcohol was to ban tobacco, which they believed "created the thirst."

The arguments employed against tobacco back then have a tediously familiar ring to them. It was claimed to be anti-social, it led to excess and addiction, it was bad for the user's health (it was attributed with causing among other things: insanity, delirium tremors, epilepsy, and impotence), and, of course, it would lead on to stronger drugs, namely "hard liquor."

"Rum-drinking will not cease," predicted a prominent anti-alcohol campaigner, the Reverend Orin Fowler, in 1833, "till tobacco-chewing, and tobacco-smoking, and snuff-taking shall cease." Fowler further sermonised that "the fierce passions of many tobacco chewers, as regards the other sex, are immensely increased by the fires kindled in their systems, and of course their cerebellums, by tobacco excitements."[5]

While the idea that tobacco smokers were a threat to women's safety might seem laughable now, it is depressing to see similar unsubstantiated claims being utilised against modern drugs like ecstasy.[6]

It is interesting to note that the "slippery slope theory" was used to attack beer, wine and cider as well as tobacco. These "soft" drinks would inevitably lead onto harder stuff such as gin, rum and whisky it was claimed, in the same way that modern-day drug prohibitionists claim that cannabis leads on to the use of stronger drugs like heroin. It's as if the same old arguments to justify prohibition continue to be passed off as some new kind of wisdom.

However, in 1830 events in Britain took a new turn. In exchange for a paltry £2 a year fee licenses for selling alcohol were dished out liberally to anyone who applied. This was widely seen as a desperate political measure passed in parliament by a deeply unpopular government of the day who were trying to cling to power by any means possible. The upshot of this? 50,000 new public houses opened up in six years and cheap beer became widely available. The urban working classes, who were labouring in factories for long hours, and in terrible conditions, could now afford to drink. Unsurprisingly, given the social conditions, many were only too relieved to be able to afford drink and "suddenly," wrote one observer of the time "everyone is drunk."[7]

The backlash was a temperance movement against alcohol. This campaigned for individuals to voluntarily "take the pledge" which tens of thousands did. As well as the backing of employers who wanted their workforce sobered up, the temperance movement had genuine support among many working class women. Too many men were spending their wages on alcohol and families were suffering as a result.

But there was never any real support for all-out alcohol prohibition. It would have been impossible to impose and had little support among politicians. One commentator of the time, Joseph Livesey, wryly suggested that *"out of 658 Members of Parliament there are probably not a dozen who would claim to be abstainers. These gentlemen have their cellars stored with liquor, have it daily on their tables, and have it introduced on every social occasion as a mark of friendship – is it likely that they would pass a Bill to prevent others enjoying the same, according to their means?"*[8]

But in the United States, where attitudes to alcohol were changing, prohibition was gaining footholds. The first modern prohibition legislation was passed in 1851 in the American state of Maine. The basic premise of the Maine Law was that all alcoholic drinks were dangerous drugs therefore they should be banned. Twelve other states followed suit and unsuccessful attempts were made to introduce similar legislation in Britain.

By 1869, a National Prohibition Party was formed in the United States which in 1890 won its first seat in the House of Representatives. All sorts of anti-alcohol measures were being introduced. In Nebraska, where alcohol was still on sale, the buying of rounds or "treating" was outlawed. In America at least, the prohibition bandwagon was gaining momentum.

Encouraged by initial successes, the prohibitionists in the States reorganised themselves this time into the Anti-Saloon League which became such a formidable force in the run-up to World War I that it could make or break political careers.

During this period, although social attitudes were sufficiently different in Britain to block the full-scale banning of alcohol, the country wasn't immune to prohibitionist tendencies. During the war years, the British Prime Minister, Lloyd George, gave serious consideration to an alcohol ban. He stated in 1916 that Britain was fighting "Germany, Austria and drink" and "the greatest of these three deadly foes is drink."[9] However, fear of social unrest persuaded him not to go ahead with the idea. Instead, after a government committee investigation, a form of harm reduction was implemented which ordered such measures as "no buying rounds" as well as reduced strength beer (two American customs). These worked well enough that by the end of the war beer consumption had dropped by a third and spirit consumption by half.

THE GREAT PROHIBITION

But it was in the United States that opponents of alcohol won their most famous victory and undertook the biggest prohibition experiment of them all.

The years after World War I ushered in a new era in America where all sorts of social changes were taking place. Like everywhere else, the 1917 October Revolution in the new Soviet Union had a profound effect among a huge layer of workers in America. A new kind of music was drifting down the Mississippi from the impoverished and disenfranchised blacks in the southern American states. And people were gathering to drink in bars where they would discuss the past, the present and what the future might hold. And since alcohol was at the centre of a lot of these social gatherings it soon came under fire.

While the good ladies of the Woman's Christian Temperance Union were at the forefront of the moral campaign against alcohol – noses tilted skywards in indignation at the behaviour of the lower social classes – behind them stood many American industrialists who wanted a more manageable workforce. The task of garnering support for prohibition was portioned out to professional ranters like Captain Richmond Pearson Hobson who claimed that alcohol "made Negroes degenerate to the level of the cannibal" and "peaceable red men became savages when they drank."[10] By 1915 Hobson was the highest paid orator on the US lecture circuit.

In 1920 the Volstead Act was passed and alcohol Prohibition (with a capital P) came into force.

Virtually overnight, the Land of the Free became a land of smugglers, gangsters, pirates, moonshine liquor, police and judicial corruption, and political chicanery, with the whole sorry mess dancing to the tune of speakeasy madness and machine guns on the streets. The names of Elliot Ness, Al Capone and Dillinger were to become synonymous with the period. The experiment had quickly turned into a disaster.

By 1923, a Washington law officer, James Beck, complained: "wholesale lawlessness virtually challenged the right of the U.S. to be master within its own household."[11]

That same year, the man in charge of enforcing prohibition, Commissioner Roy Haynes, was honest enough to reveal some of the dire consequences of Prohibition. In the first five months of 1923 coroners' inquests had found that a hundred people had died from drinking "bootleg hooch."[12] Haynes felt this was a gross underestimate. But as well as the health hazards of illegal drinking, corruption was becoming endemic. In his book, *Prohibition Inside Out*, Haynes admitted that forty-three of his own agents had been found guilty of illegalities in Philadelphia alone, with those caught "doubtless but a fraction of those who are guilty." It was becoming apparent that the gangsters were buying up influence and power with the vast profits they were making from selling bootleg liquor.

A famous trial in Indiana at the time illustrated the far-reaching tentacles of corruption. A proprietor of an illegal drinking establishment was caught paying protection money. Those paid off were found to have included: "the mayor, the sheriff, a judge of the city court, the prosecuting attorney of the county, a former sheriff, a former prosecuting attorney, a detective sergeant, a justice of the peace, an influential lawyer, and former deputy sheriffs, detectives, policemen, petty lawyers, bartenders, cabaret singers and notorious women."[13]

This was in a relatively small town in Indiana only three years into Prohibition. It gives an indication of the sheer scale of the law-and-order meltdown that must have happened in cities like Chicago by the time Prohibition was finally repealed in 1933. By then America was screaming to be freed from the influence of the territory wars, the killings, the shootings, the gangsters, and their poisonous interference in public life.

Nowadays, nobody touts alcohol prohibition as a serious proposition because it didn't work in practice. It was acknowledged to have undermined the social peace, led to official corruption, an escalation of crime, and a breakdown of law and order. Unfortunately, the prohibitionists didn't extend this line of logic to other drugs. The gangsters and crime syndicates, who had grown very rich and powerful from the Prohibition years, did however, and were already moving into this lucrative area.

Throughout the nineteenth century in both America and Europe there were no legal constrictions placed on the sale of opium or any of its derivatives. Opiate-based medicines were in wide use for all sorts of ailments with brands such as *Mrs Winslow's Soothing Syrup for Children* and *Dover's Powder* being household names. Although addiction to the medicine's pleasant side-effects was reasonably common it wasn't considered a problem. In America, for instance, in the 1880s you could stay high on morphine for less than 5 cents a day – meaning addicts weren't out mugging their neighbours for the price of a fix.[14]

Most people took opium and its derivatives in solution forms such as laudanum. Opium smoking was almost exclusively practised by the Chinese.

Then came the economic depression of 1875 when jobs became scarce and the white American labour movement cast its accusative eyes towards the Chinese. The Chinese were blamed for taking their jobs and undermining their wages as cost-cutting bosses used them as a source of cheap labour.

The Chinese and all aspects of their culture came under siege. Opium smoking became "the Chinese vice." All sorts of ludicrous tales were told of prostitutes being tricked into opium smoking and being abducted by "insidious yellow fiends" into a white slave trade.[15] Racist myths led to San Francisco passing America's first anti-narcotic laws in 1875 when opium smoking was banned. By the time the Harrison Narcotics Act came into effect in 1915 – which prohibited the use of drugs such as opiates and cocaine for non-medical purposes – 27 American states had already outlawed the smoking of opium. Those with moral, religious or ideological axes to grind about drug-taking hid behind the smoke-screen of anti-Chinese racism. Employers too believed that their source of cheap Chinese labour might be undermined if they were smoking opium all day.

However, the attempt at opium prohibition failed in practice. In 1870 the amount of opium which came into the United States was around 21,000 pounds in weight. This trebled to more than 64,000 pounds by 1890.[16] Smoking of opium was merely driven underground.

The Harrison Narcotics Act had ushered in another disastrous chapter in the history of drug prohibition in America. When drugs such as morphine and heroin were banned it was left to the police rather than doctors to determine what was "medical use." Doctors who prescribed morphine or heroin to addicts in what was known as a maintenance dose were arrested, faced jail sentences, and lost their jobs. Addicts were forced to go to underworld sources for their drugs and, not surprisingly, the underworld was quick to respond to a lucrative new market.

By 1918, the number of addicts in America had risen to around a million and the illegal opiates market was now as large as the legal traffic.[17] America went down a familiar road as it tried to get to grips with the problem it had inadvertently created. There was tougher sentencing, harsh new laws, and in 1924, the importing of heroin was banned.

Yet all of this actually exacerbated the problem. Many in the medical profession were shaking their heads in exasperation at the foolishness of the prohibitionists. The Illinois Medical Journal in June 1926 complained that the "well-meaning blunderers" who had passed the Act had ensured that those who dealt in heroin could now "make double the money from the poor unfortunates upon whom they prey."

In a damning indictment of prohibition the respected figure of August Vollmer, a Chief of Police in Berkeley, California, as well a former President of the International Association of Chiefs of Police, explained what had happened:

> *"Stringent laws, spectacular police drives, vigorous prosecution and imprisonment of addicts and peddlers have proved not only useless and enormously expensive as means of correcting this evil, but they are also unjustifiably and unbelievably cruel in their application to the unfortunate drug victims. Repression has driven this vice underground and produced the narcotic smugglers and supply agents, who have grown wealthy out of this evil practice and who, by devious methods, have stimulated traffic in drugs. Finally, and not the least of the evils associated with repression, the helpless addict has been forced to resort to crime in order to get money for the drug."*[18]

It was Vollmer's contention that drug addiction was a medical problem not a police problem.

Up until 1914, Britain had had a similar problem arising from addiction to opiates. Like America, doctors were being blamed for ill-advised prescribing habits and there was a boom in opiate-based patent medicines. However, Britain went down a significantly different road in the way it dealt with its addicts. A commission was set up by the Ministry of Health under Sir Humphrey Rolleston which reported on how the Harrison Act worked in practice. One of its members, Dr Harry Campbell, reported:

> *"It appears that not only has the Harrison law failed to diminish the number of drug-takers – some contend, indeed, that it has actually worsened it; for without curtailing the supply of the drug it has sent the price up tenfold, and this has had the effect of impoverishing the poorer class of addicts and reducing them to a condition of such abject misery as to render them incapable of gaining an honest livelihood."*[19]

The Rolleston Committee recommended that doctors should be able to continue prescribing heroin to addicts who *"while capable of leading a useful and fairly normal life as long as he takes a certain non-progressive quantity, usually small, of the drug of addiction, ceases to be able to do so when the regular allowance is withdrawn."* This prescribing of a maintenance dose of heroin (or other drugs) became generally known as "the British method" to differentiate it from what had happened in the U.S. And it made a world of difference. A significant heroin problem didn't begin here until 1967 when Britain finally backed down and adopted the disastrous American methods.[20]

INTERNATIONAL ATTEMPTS
AT DRUG PROHIBITION

With the formation of the League of Nations in 1920 there began a series of attempts to regulate the production, sale and consumption of narcotic drugs on an international basis. But far from reaching universal agreement on the best course to halt the use of these drugs, the succession of treaties, agreements and international undertakings ended in failure as member countries wriggled and squirmed to protect their own economic interests. None more so than Britain which had control of the world's biggest opium growing areas within the borders of its largest colony, India.

British colonial policy in India in the first three decades of this century was pretty much a continuation of the policy of the nineteenth century. This had been the period of the infamous Opium Wars which saw British ships sailing down the Yangtse River shelling the Chinese in order to force them into buying British opium. In the name of free trade.

Britain had no intention of giving up the vast source of revenue which the opium fields of India generated. When the young

Ghandi, in 1921, denounced opium as "that other oppressor" and called for a campaign against it, his followers were arrested by the British colonialists on charges of "undermining the revenue."[21] As well as Britain, other countries such as Holland, France and Turkey, all had a vested interest in the continuation of the opium trade. They continually evaded and manoeuvred their way out of controls. By the mid-1930s, with the rise of Hitler and Mussolini in Europe, and with the Japanese invasion of northern China, all attempted agreements on international drug control fell to pieces.

In 1961, America would finally get all the member states of the United Nations to sign up to the UN's Single Convention on Narcotic Drugs. But even this proved unworkable in practice as many member states had no intention of losing the revenue that illicit drugs brought. It this Agreement (and its update in 1988) that is still cited as one of the main reasons why no member country of the United Nations can break ranks and end drug prohibition within its own borders.

CANNABIS OR "MARIHUANA" PROHIBITION

America's attempts to outlaw opiates and cocaine were repeated with other drugs. First of all cannabis was effectively outlawed in 1937 when the U.S. Treasury introduced a Federal Marihuana Bill which put it into the same category as all the other drugs controlled by the Harrison Act.

The original reasons for the outlawing of cannabis tell us more about the sort of people who wanted it banned than anything about the alleged dangers of the drug.

Cannabis is unique among recreational drugs in that the plant that it comes from – cannabis hemp – is also one of the most versatile and useful plants on the face of the planet. It can grow virtually anywhere and quickly. Cannabis hemp is a natural fibre which has any amount of uses. Rope, canvas (the word is derived from a Dutch word for cannabis), cloth, linen, and paper, are all products of the hemp plant. The cellulose hurd which makes up to 80 per cent of the cannabis hemp plant can also be turned into environmentally-friendly products such as soaps, oils, engine fluid and even plastics.

In 1937, when the Marihuana Tax Act was passed, natural hemp products were in competition with the new synthetic fibres which came from the petrochemical industry, such as nylon and rayon. The new law forbade the growing of hemp even for non-drug uses.

An American company who took advantage of this new law to establish a virtual monopoly on the production of man-made fibres was the (then) munitions maker, DuPont.

In 1937, prior to the banning of cannabis, DuPont's Annual Report to its stockholders urged investment towards petrochemical-based synthetic products. Sixty years later, DuPont are America's single largest producer of man-made fibres. Interestingly, the chief financial backer of DuPont in 1937 was Mellon Bank of Pittsburgh. Andrew Mellon, of Mellon Bank, when working for The Treasury in 1931, appointed Harry J. Anslinger to be head of the newly-organised Federal Bureau of Narcotics and Dangerous Drugs, a position he held for 31 years. Anslinger was America's most vocal crusader for alcohol and cannabis prohibition. Harry Anslinger was also, by coincidence, Andrew Mellon's son-in-law.[22]

Was this a conspiracy by the petrochemical industry against hemp products? Well, to this day, it is *still* illegal to grow cannabis hemp plants in America for the production of natural fibres – despite the fact that it is a straightforward process to grow the crop without the active drug ingredient THC.

While the industrialists with vested interests lurked in the background, lobbying and pulling strings, chief prohibitionist Harry J. Anslinger led the campaign from the front, trying to manipulate public opinion against cannabis users by all sorts of dishonest means. As allies he had people like the newspaper baron William Randolph Hearst – "Citizen Kane" – who for the first three decades of this century had conducted a vicious campaign of racists smears against the "lazy marihuana-smoking Mexicans." Hearst's almost psychopathic hatred of Mexicans stemmed from 1898, when Mexicans under Pancho Villa seized 800,000 acres of his prime Mexican timberlands.[23] It was Hearst who began using the word "marihuana" to describe cannabis. This was an old Mexican word for cannabis and one which Hearst used in a derogatory way to try and stigmatise the previously considered benign cannabis hemp plant.

Hearst jumped onto the prohibition bandwagon with glee. Some of his more moderate newspaper headlines screamed: *"Marihuana makes fiends of boys in 30 days"*, *"Hasheesh goads users to blood-lust"* and *"Hotel clerk identifies marihuana smoker as 'wild gunman' arrested for shootings."*[24] These headlines in the Hearst press were used as factual evidence against cannabis by Anslinger.

Anslinger was then quoted in another of Hearst's paper telling people that *"if the hideous monster Frankenstein came face to face with the monster marihuana he would drop dead of fright."*[25]

Hearst and Anslinger didn't draw the line at racially insulting Mexicans. Hearst's newspapers depicted blacks under the influence of "marihuana" listening to "voodoo-satanic" music – jazz – before going out to rape white women. Previously Hearst had claimed that cocaine had turned blacks into rapists but since coke was banned by this time cannabis was conveniently inserted into the old racist propaganda.

White, god-fearing, all-American youth were under threat from this black man's drug claimed Anslinger and it had to be stopped.

Statistics were wheeled out to prove that – in the words of Anslinger testifying to Congress in 1937 – "marihuana is the most violence-causing drug in the history of mankind." He even related to congress a story of how an axe-murderer had smoked a joint *four days* before he committed a murder. Significantly, the congressional committee on cannabis use was dominated by representatives from the conservative southern states and Harry Anslinger's racist diatribes against cannabis users found a receptive audience.

Incredible as it seems now, this was how cannabis became a banned substance: a combination of racism, vested economic interests of both the petrochemical and pharmaceutical industries, and an attack on popular youth culture. (Hoover even banned jazz from the radio!) It wasn't until 1948 that Anslinger changed his tune and started trying to justify the ban on cannabis in terms of health and the drug's supposed capacity to turn users into pacifist-zombies (up until then cannabis had supposedly been the mind-deranging energy-fuel of homicidal axe-murderers, etc.).

Prohibition didn't curtail the use of cannabis. As an exercise in social control it was self-defeating. In 1937 an estimated 60,000 Americans smoked cannabis. The change in the law merely turned users into outlaws and the popularity of cannabis spread like wildfire in the years that followed. After half a decade of prohibition it was estimated that one in three Americans had tried it at least once and between 10 and 20 per cent of Americans smoke cannabis regularly.[26]

Using similar methods, LSD would later be outlawed in the Sixties. Again, prohibitionists would use equally ludicrous tales of young girls jumping to their death out of windows under the influence of the hallucinogenic drug. (So often was this story retold that even today it is still believed despite there not being one single documented case of it ever having happened.)

In conservative minds, LSD and other psychoactive substances were often associated with such Sixties phenomena as the movement against American intervention in Vietnam; the black consciousness movement; nuclear disarmament; women's liberation; beatniks and hippies; the seemingly alien fashions and long hair; and as always, the music. These were the real targets of those who attacked the drugs. It was social change they feared and they thought that it could be halted if the drug culture at its centre could be suppressed. It was a futile but blatant attempt to impose social control on young people.

The banning of recreational substances has always gone hand in hand with an attack on the culture in which they were taken. There is no space here to go into every detail about the way that techno music, acid house, the rave scene, warehouse parties, and all aspects of dance culture were attacked by a Conservative government (with opposition support). Government legislation attacked not just the drug ecstasy, which was an integral part of the scene, but even included legislation against illegal gatherings which played "loud, repetitive beats"! If this had happened in Victorian times we would have laughed at the absurdity of it. But is is enshrined in British law in 1997. Evidently, an older generation of conservatives still relies on the swing of police batons to suppress a youth culture they don't understand.

The justification for this authoritarian onslaught against dance culture was led by a hysterical anti-drug campaign in the media. (Matthew Collin in his essential book *Altered States* gives a fascinating history of this.)

The fervour of the prohibitionists against recreational drugs shows little sign of abating. Even as I put the finishing touches to this book the British government have been busy banning such relatively harmless substances as herbal highs. Yet not once has any government stopped to ask the most pertinent question: *Does drug prohibition actually work?*

THE WAR AGAINST DRUGS HAS BEEN LOST: IT'S OFFICIAL

Thirty-six years have passed since the signing of the United Nations agreement in 1961 which bound all the U.N. member states to follow America's lead on drug prohibition. Thirty-six years is a sufficiently long time by any standards to determine whether the policy of drug prohibition has been successful.

The agencies created to combat illegal drug use have grown in size and multiplied in a way never imagined back then. In the U.S. alone it is conservatively estimated that $15 billion a year is spent by the government on financing 57 different departments and agencies involved in their anti-drug strategy.[1]

The full amount expended yearly by all the governments involved in the war against drugs can only be guessed at. Because of the covert nature of these operations accurate figures will never be forthcoming. Annually, it would almost certainly be more than the £69 billion development aid which the United Nations earmarked in 1996 for the world's poorest countries.[2]

The war against drugs is a multi-national industry in its own right. It is an industry which has hierarchical structures, power bases internationally, and a vast army of employees – many of them literally armed to the teeth – with networks of undercover agents in every country in the world. It has at its disposal high-tech surveillance equipment such as satellites in space which can detect not just where the opium fields of Asia are situated but are so sophisticated they can detect which council house in Fife is using UV lights to grow a few dozen plants of cannabis in the attic! Vast networks of police informers have been established and powers such as those used to tap telephones of suspected drug traffickers are in place and are used freely. It is reasonable to assume that if the war against drugs was winnable then there would be hard evidence by now to show that it is happening.

THE WORLD DRUG REPORT

On 27th June 1997, the United Nations released The World Drug Report. It had been compiled by the United Nations Drug Control Programme (UNDCP). It had been produced to give an idea of the global picture in the war against drugs: drawing together information on production, trafficking, consumption, health effects of drugs, and efforts made to tackle them. Its findings are nothing short of astounding and should have been openly discussed in parliaments the world over. Any politician who wants to continue waging a war against drugs should be asked to explain this report's findings.

The UNDCP report estimated that the world trade in illicit drugs now stands at $400 billion (£250 billion) per annum. This is so staggering I'll repeat it in case any reader thinks this is a misprint. The UNDCP report estimated that the world trade in illicit drugs now stands at $400 billion (£250 billion) per annum. This accounts for a colossal *eight per cent (8%)* of international trade. To put this into perspective the illegal drug trade is now bigger that the international trade in iron, steel or motor vehicles.

As if this wasn't a heavy enough nail in the drug prohibition coffin there was even worse to come. The UNDCP reported that despite all of the international efforts to hit the drug trade at its source – ie at the areas of production – between 1985 and 1996 world production of opium had *trebled* and world production of coca leaf had *doubled*. These are the plants responsible for the synthesis of heroin and cocaine. This surge in production was reflected in a drop in the worldwide street prices of these drugs: again indicating clearly that significantly larger quantities of these drugs were hitting the streets than ever before.

This report – for the first ever time – estimated the numbers of drug users internationally. It calculated that 141,000,000 people had used cannabis in the previous year (around 3 per cent of the world's adult population – which is food for thought in itself); with an estimated 30,000,000 amphetamine users; 13,000,000 cocaine users; and 8,000,000 heroin users. The report also warned of a growing globalisation of the illegal drug trade with consumption growing rapidly in places such as Africa and the former Soviet Union where drug epidemics have been predicted.

These findings are remarkable. After decades of attempting to stamp out drug use through internationally co-ordinated drug prohibition policies – using up vast national resources in every country involved – an objective view of this report can only come to one honest conclusion: *The war against drugs has been lost.*

You might expect the authors of such a report, along with alerted politicians, to be holding their hands up and admitting: "Okay, we tried our best, but it's obvious that prohibition has failed to even contain the use of drugs. Maybe there's another way of tackling this problem."

But you'd be wrong. Despite referring to possible alternative options such as legalisation, the UN report surprisingly concluded that the best way forward was: crop eradication in the drug-growing countries; destruction of chemical production facilities; interdicting drug traffickers; and reducing demand through drug education programmes. In other words, more of the same.

Within weeks of the UN report being published both British and American governments announced that they would be intensifying their efforts to fight the drug barons internationally.

Robin Cook, the British Foreign Secretary, specifically targeted the opium producers of Burma when he announced:

> *"There is evidence that the military government of Burma connives with the drugs trade. We want to work with the responsible members of south-east Asia to curb production and trade in drugs. We will be using all our assets, including the work of our intelligent services, for whom work against the drugs trade becomes increasingly important as they free up resources from the end of the Cold War."* [3]

Has this approach got any realistic chance of success? Or will it be another example of throwing good public money after bad? The facts speak for themselves.

Burma is the single largest producer of opium in the south-east of Asia. One man, General Khun Sa, the world's most powerful drugs baron, is in control of a £2 billion-a-year industry which controls an estimated 60 per cent of the heroin that floods into the West. He has a private army of 20,000 followers and has been accused of cutting a straight deal with the Burmese government to continue the lucrative trade in opium and heroin. Yet the opium trade in Burma doesn't only rely upon corrupt state officials. Poor farmers throughout Burma rely on the £60 a kilo that their opium harvest brings.[4]

Detective Chief Inspector Ron Clarke, a former senior member of the Greater Manchester Drugs Squad, hit the nail on the head when he explained:

"The pressure on the poor farmers in the Third World is intense. Given the personal choice of risking seeing your children die if you plant a coffee crop, or guaranteeing a good cash return for cannabis plants or opium poppies, it is easy to see how the problems arise." [5]

As is often the case, the impoverished farmers are loyal to their paymasters in the drug trade as a result. It is opium poppies and not the wishes of foreign governments that put bread on their tables.

So the question needs to be asked: How on earth does Robin Cook expect to halt opium production in Burma? Or anywhere else for that matter. An all-out military invasion has been ruled out. Economic sanctions would be impossible to enforce since there are so many drug-producing countries. Even a covert operation to assassinate General Khun Sa would make little difference as he'd simply be replaced by another ruthless drug baron.

Ultimately it is the supply-led economics of drug production which suggest that this approach is a futile one. Even if by some miracle opium production in Burma was significantly reduced the slack would simply be taken up by an increase in production somewhere else. It's a Catch-22 situation.

The United States has discovered similar problems with Mexico. It has been estimated that more than half of the £50 billion worth of drugs which comes into the United States does so across this border.[6] It is big business. America's "drug tsar" Barry McCaffrey, a former army general, has tried to halt the flood of drugs coming across the Mexican border by collaborating with the Mexican authorities. McCaffrey told the Dallas Morning News:

"It is a long struggle, but one that both countries are willing to confront." Yet in an astonishing admission in the same interview, he added: "Nobody would argue the way we're doing it makes any sense."[7]

McCaffrey has found that the huge profits made in the illegal drug trade have corrupted the law enforcement agencies on both sides of the border. US Intelligence officials believe that Mexican drug traffickers take in $10 billion a year and spend up to 60 per cent on bribes.[8] Mr McCaffrey's main ally in the cross-border war against drugs was Mexico's drug enforcement chief, General Jesus Gutiérrez Rebello. McCaffrey described him as "an honest man and a no-nonsense field commander."[9] Yet General Rebello has subsequently been arrested and charged with working for Amado Carillo Fuentes. Fuentes, whose death in July '97 instigated a fierce and bloody battle between rival factions, was Mexico's most feared and powerful drugs baron. Rebello was even accused of helping Fuentes pursue a rival drugs gang.

In other drug-producing countries like Columbia, Peru, Venezuela and Bolivia complicity between the drug cartels and government forces is rife. In many cases, both at national and local levels, it is difficult to see where one stops and the other begins. The principals of democracy and free government are being poisoned by the illegal trade in drugs. And the harsh truth of the matter is that there is nothing anyone can do about it as long as the drug trade is kept lucratively illegal. These people have both the guns and influence to keep themselves untouchable.

Even in Communist Party-controlled Vietnam government officials are implicated in drug-related crime. In January '97 high ranking members of the interior ministry were arrested and implicated over the arrest of two Laotian drug traffickers. Street corner and shooting gallery heroin abuse is escalating in the country. One commentator hit the nail on the head when he said:

> *"That conservative Vietnam should be vulnerable to the high tide of drug-related corruption in south-east Asia says as much about the increasing strength and sophistication of international criminals as it does about local law and order."* [10]

It isn't just in the poorer third world countries where the influence of the international drug syndicates casts its all-pervasive web. A whole book could be filled with the cases of American and European police officers, secret service agents, politicians, judicial figures and government officials who have resigned or been prosecuted because of their links with the criminal drug gangs. These "bad apples" often decide that their official salary is no match to the riches on offer from the drug gangs. Sometimes more "persuasive" methods are used to buy influence. Such as blackmail, terror and intimidation.

There is an arrogant Western attitude that it's just the officials and government agencies of Third World countries who are implicated in the drug trade. If this was the case, then why did General Maurice Belleux, the former chief of French intelligence for Indochina, state that the CIA was involved in the opium trade during the Vietnam War just as their French counterparts had been before them.[11] Belleux told investigative writer Alfred McCoy that his agency had controlled Indochina's illicit drug trade and used it to finance clandestine operations against Communist guerrillas. He suggested to McCoy that a trip to Saigon would reveal that American intelligence was involved in the opium trade. The French paratroop commander Colonel Roger Trinquier confirmed both the general's information and his suggestion. Alfred McCoy was to spend the greater part of his life investigating CIA complicity in the global drug trade – at great personal risk – and his subsequent book on the subject, *The Politics of Heroin*, has enough hard evidence to convince even the most sceptical of readers that this was no wild conspiracy theory.

Closer to home, a recent example of the pernicious influence of the illegal drugs trade has come to light in Scotland. An investigation was launched in July 1997 into events in the Paisley area – events that have already seen one Scottish Member of Parliament, Gordon McMaster, commit suicide because of smears made against him, and another, Irene Adams, claim that she has had death threats.[12] Both had spoken out against what they claimed were the influence of the drug barons in their local area. An investigation into goings-on in Paisley has so far unearthed a local government funded company, FCB Security, with gross financial irregularities and missing sums of money amounting to £320,000 – which could even be as high as £1.6million according to *The Scotsman*.[13] Irene Adams MP has claimed that this company was linked to laundering drug money.[14]

At the time of writing, the local Labour Party in Paisley has been shut down since 1995 because of irregularities surrounding attempts to deselect Irene Adams and Gordon McMaster prior to the last General Election. Senior Labour politicians named in McMaster's suicide note are, at the time of writing, suspended from the party and under investigation.[15]

The whole affair has become synonymous with the corruption that exists in public life, as well as the influence that the black market in drugs exerts on the town, particularly in the deprived Ferguslie Park estate in Paisley. Ferguslie Park has been at the centre of an ongoing and particularly vicious drugs war which has already claimed the lives of a number of people in recent years. Whatever the outcome of ongoing investigations it has become apparent that the influence of the illegal drugs trade is not only undermining law and order in the area but undermining the foundations of democracy itself. And this isn't far-flung Columbia or Burma. This is Scotland 1997.

DRUG PROHIBITION IN THE UK – THE GENERAL TRENDS

If drug prohibition was working there would be evidence of this when we examine the yearly trends of indicators such as the number of drug seizures made and the number of drug offenders dealt with. We should reasonably expect to see both trends register a steady drop in the number of seizures and offenders as drug prohibition succeeds in its objectives.

DRUG SEIZURES

In 1996 British customs officers and police seized drugs valued at £500 million weighing 80 tonnes.[16] This was a record high. The volume and value of drug seizures for that year was up by almost 10 per cent on the previous year. In 1995 the seizure of £457 million worth of drugs weighing 55 tonnes was up 9 per cent on the previous year.[17] And that was up on the year before. The trend is relentlessly upwards. This is in line with the trend in the number of drug seizures by police and customs which has risen from 10,648 in 1975 to 115,000 in 1995.[18]

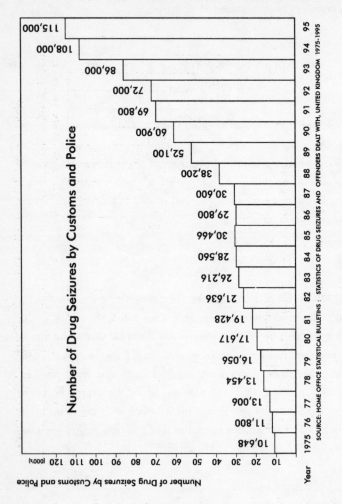

Number of Drug Seizures by Customs and Police

Year	Number of Drug Seizures by Customs and Police (000's)
1975	10,648
76	11,800
77	13,006
78	13,454
79	16,056
80	17,617
81	19,428
82	21,636
83	26,216
84	28,560
85	30,466
86	29,800
87	30,600
88	38,200
89	52,100
90	60,900
91	69,800
92	72,000
93	86,000
94	108,000
95	115,000

SOURCE: HOME OFFICE STATISTICAL BULLETINS : STATISTICS OF DRUG SEIZURES AND OFFENDERS DEALT WITH, UNITED KINGDOM 1975-1995

NUMBER OF DRUG SEIZURES FROM 1975 TO 1995[19]

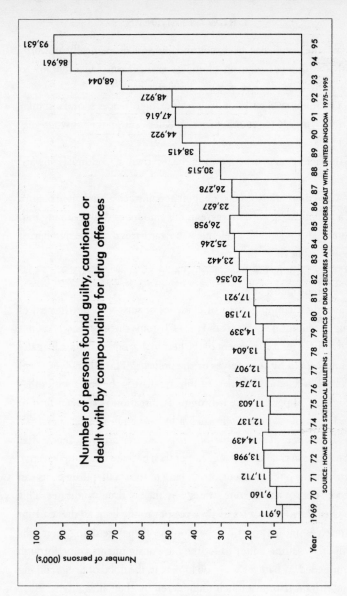

Number of persons found guilty, cautioned or dealt with by compounding for drug offences

Year	Number of persons (000's)
1969	6,911
70	9,160
71	11,712
72	13,998
73	14,439
74	12,137
75	11,603
76	12,754
77	12,907
78	13,604
79	14,339
80	17,158
81	17,921
82	20,356
83	23,442
84	25,246
85	26,958
86	23,627
87	26,278
88	30,515
89	38,415
90	44,922
91	47,616
92	48,927
93	68,044
94	86,961
95	93,631

SOURCE: HOME OFFICE STATISTICAL BULLETINS : STATISTICS OF DRUG SEIZURES AND OFFENDERS DEALT WITH, UNITED KINGDOM 1975-1995

NUMBER OF DRUG OFFENDERS DEALT WITH FROM 1969 TO 1995.[20]

Again the trend has been continually and dramatically upwards with the number of drug offenders rising from 7,000 in 1969 to 94,000 in 1995 – a rise of over 1,300 per cent.[21]

The number of cases of drug trafficking offences shows a similar pattern. In 1996 the number rose by 8 per cent on the previous year to 11,200 cases.[22]

In fact, every drug statistic has shown a continual upward trend.

All of these statistics taken together paint a clear and vivid picture of a relentless upward increase in the amount of drugs coming into Britain and an equally relentless upward trend in the number of people using these drugs.

Drug prohibition has clearly failed to even contain drug use, never mind put a stop to it.

Another damning piece of evidence against the effectiveness of drug prohibition comes from H.M. Customs themselves who admit that only around 10 per cent of the heroin that enters Britain illegally is intercepted by themselves or the police.[23] The other 90 per cent gets to the intended market of the street. It is the same with other drugs. A 10 per cent loss through confiscation is chicken-feed to the big crime syndicates in such a lucrative tax-free business.

More often than not, the big drug seizures are only made after tip-offs from rival drug gangs rather than because of astute detective work by the police and customs. Many of the smaller drug busts can also be part of a deliberate strategy by the big drug syndicates. This is when they throw a small-time courier to the lions so that corrupt detectives and customs officials look as if they're doing their jobs properly. All the better to let the big consignments come through unimpeded. Whatever way you look at it, the flood of drugs coming into Britain is pretty much unhindered by their illegality.

DRUGS IN PRISON

When you consider the extent of drug use in the prison system the failures of customs and police are put into perspective. Scotland has 22 prisons with a prison population of around 6000 inmates. These prisons are surrounded by high walls, perimeter fences and rolls of razor wire. They have CCTV systems, sniffer dogs, perimeter patrols, intelligence-gathering among inmates, random cell-searches, strip searches, mandatory drug testing, and over 4500 staff working for the Scottish Prison Service. Yet in his annual report, H.M. Chief Inspector of Prisons for Scotland, Clive Fairweather, stated that 80 per cent of the prisoners in Scottish jails were using drugs.[24] In one prison, Glenochil, an investigation discovered that around 90 per cent of the prison's 370 adult inmates were using drugs, and more disturbingly, up to 70 per cent of inmates there regularly take heroin.[25] The report singled out Perth, Barlinnie and Aberdeen as having the worst problems, worse even than Glenochil. Other prisons such as Low Moss, Saughton and the women's prison at Corton Vale all have well-documented evidence of the extent of illegal drug use.

This leads to one inescapable conclusion. Namely, if a tightly regulated system such as a prison cannot be policed effectively for illicit drug use, then what chance is there of enforcing prohibition in a free and open society such as ours?

THE SOCIAL COST OF DRUG PROHIBITION

As well as the violence, intimidation and corruption that come with the illegal drug trade, there is a heavy price paid by the rest of society for keeping drugs illegal. This comes mainly in the form of drug-related property crimes, but to this can also be added the cost of maintaining expensive anti-drugs organisations like regional drug squads and the various departments of MI5, as well as the social cost of the erosion of civil liberties that follows as these under-cover agencies increase the scope of their surveillance and operations.

In a campaign analysed in the following chapter, *Scotland Against Drugs* ran billboard ads during July '97 which stated that 70 per cent of all property crime was drug-related. The figure may be an exaggeration and the statement misleading but it would be wrong to dismiss it out of hand as just more anti-drugs propaganda. Heroin users who are unemployed and unable to kick their addiction will have little alternative except to turn to shoplifting, housebreaking, street robbery and car crime.

A Home Office report released in May '97 claimed that one in five crimes are committed by people on heroin. Home Secretary, Jack Straw seized upon its publication (a lucky coincidence?) to announce the creation of a U.S.-style "drugs tsar". He commented: *"The first thing to really establish in the public's mind is this profound link between drugs and crime."* [26] (This statement would have been more accurate if Straw had said "the profound link between *addictive drugs like heroin* and *property crime."* Yet again this shows the mistake of trying to reduce the complex issue of drugs down to snappy media soundbites).

This Home Office report calculated that property worth around £1.3 billion is stolen annually to pay for heroin addiction.[27] Other reports, however, suggest even this may be a gross underestimate. The Select Committee on Scottish Affairs when investigating the link between drug addiction and crime discovered that a whole parallel economy existed in many areas based on shoplifting and housebreaking. It estimated that goods valued at £936 million were stolen every year to pay for drug addiction. On a UK-wide basis that would be around £8-10 billion.

This was more in line with a report drawn up by drug workers and health experts in Glasgow in 1996 – and these were people who had no vested interest in scapegoating drug users for rising crime – which estimated that as much as £500 million worth of crimes were committed annually to pay for heroin addiction in the Strathclyde region alone.[28]

Their figure was based on the region's estimated 8,500 injecting addicts needing to spend on average £300 per week to feed their habits. (NB: Stolen goods get on average about a fifth of their actual value on the black market. The overall figure has decreased since then with the falling street price of heroin and as more injecting addicts go onto methadone maintenance programmes.)

Although the price of heroin has fallen recently, it is still grossly inflated way beyond the production price of less than £2 per gram at the UK's only licensed heroin production laboratories in Edinburgh. The black market price is determined by the drug cartels and addicts have no choice but to pay it. And the higher the price of the heroin then the more crime that is committed to feed this addiction.

It is another simple but very real equation: the black market in drugs means increased property crime for everyone else.

NEW LABOUR, NEW APPROACH TO DRUGS?

So what has been the new government's response to all of this? An admission that the war against drugs has been lost both at home and abroad? A rethink on drug prohibition? Fresh ideas?

Predictably, it's been a case of Carry On Constable. Tony Blair announced soon after he was elected: *"I want to breathe new life into the battle against drugs. We will hit hard on drugs and the drugs trade."* [29] Any thoughts of taking drugs out of the hands of the black market was immediately quashed. The appointment of a US-style "drugs tsar" to co-ordinate and lead yet another war on drugs was duly announced by the Blair administration. Yet again it's time to sit back and watch as a new government goes through the motions of flexing its law-and-order muscles so that it can be *seen* to be doing something – even if what it is doing has failed many times before.

The Blair administration is infatuated with Clinton-style answers to crime and drug use. The "zero tolerance" approach is the current favourite. In America this policy of "three strikes and you're out" combined with savage sentencing has been a disaster. 440,000 people are in local jails. 87,000 people are in federal prisons. 2.7 million are on probation and more than 500,000 are on parole.[30] In the year ending 30 June '95, nearly 90,000 prison inmates were added to the U.S. prison population, of which an astounding 60 per cent were being held on drug charges. The vast majority of those are for low-level, non-violent drug offences. Is this what we want in Britain? The wholesale criminalisation of young people? A poster put on the side of buses by *Scotland Against Drugs* said: *Drug Dealers? There's plenty room for more inside*. Maybe they should have consulted with HM Prisons first. The prisons are full and overcrowded.

The black market in drugs is almost classic pyramid selling. Imprison one dealer at any level in the pyramid and another one takes their place. The further up the pyramid you go, the more untouchable the dealers get. The profits are massive and there is so much unemployment, low wages and poverty around that there is an inexhaustible supply of replacements for those near the bottom who do get caught. When will politicians learn that cracking down on drug dealers doesn't work. Ian Hamilton, a prominent Scottish QC, caustically remarked: *"They've been stamping on drugs for so long they should be given a boot allowance."* [31]

The problem with the Carry On Constable approach is that it's not the drug barons at the top who suffer. For them it's Carry On

Regardless. It's everyone else that suffers. The ordinary people who don't use drugs but live in areas blighted by drug-related crime. And the drug users themselves who are turned into criminals, continually harassed, and have to go to the black market to buy suspect drugs at inflated prices with all the potential health risks this may entail.

It all begs the question: *Who then is benefiting from drug prohibition?* Obviously the crime syndicates, gangsters and drug dealers are happy about the situation. They're making a lot of money. Then there are the professional anti-drugs campaigners, the police drug squads, and the shadowy organisations affiliated to MI5 who are all kept rolling along on the public subsidy gravy train. No small salaries there. And then there are the alcohol and tobacco industries which get a free run at the legal drugs market which generates billions of pounds for them in profits. (One UK brewing company alone, Scottish & Newcastle, had total sales in 1996/7 of £3.35 billion with pre-tax profits of £374.1 million.)[32] But apart from these vested interests the present situation benefits virtually no one except the drug barons. It is the worst of all possible worlds.

The case for taking drugs out of the black market and regulating their sale is so overwhelming that the question that really needs to be asked is not *Should it be done?* but *How should it be done?*

SCOTLAND AGAINST DRUGS?

"A vital part of the £1 million campaign is to persuade young people that drug-taking is morally and socially wrong."

DAVID MACAULEY, *SAD* CAMPAIGN DIRECTOR, 3rd MAY 96[1]

"Education on its own has been proved time and time again to be ineffective. You can't educate a kid to death. If you don't give him something useful to do with his time and he lives in an area where drugs are endemic, all the education in the world will not protect him."

DAVID MACAULEY, *SAD* CAMPAIGN DIRECTOR, 10th JULY 96[2]

"Scotland Against Drugs isn't a Just-Say-No campaign. It's about education, the provision of alternatives for young people, and harm reduction."

DAVID MACAULEY, *SAD* CAMPAIGN DIRECTOR, 13th FEB 97[3]

"There are agencies like Enhance for example whose work we actively support because we realise there's a place for that type of information . . . and Crew 2000 do go into clubs, they do provide this information for clubbers and we'd back them on that, we've no problem with that at all."

DAVID MACAULEY, *SAD* CAMPAIGN DIRECTOR, 21st MAY 97[4]

"Something needs to be done about those groups who peddle the myth that drugs can be taken safely."

DAVID MACAULEY, *SAD* CAMPAIGN DIRECTOR, 21st JUNE 97[5]

From time to time governments launch high-profile anti-drugs campaigns. They do it with sincerity because they know how much people are concerned about drug use. According to recent surveys, drug use has consistently been cited as one of the top four social concerns. Governments have to pay attention to these concerns. And act on them. But rarely is any research done beforehand on whether these anti-drugs campaigns are effective or not. It is assumed that if people are being warned about the dangers of taking drugs and the police are cracking down on drug dealers then this is the best that can be done. But is it?

During the 1980s the Conservative government launched a Heroin-Screws-You-Up campaign which was their response to the alarming rise in the use of heroin at the time. Heroin was causing real problems in many areas of the country and with the spread of the HIV/AIDS virus something had to be done.

Similarly, in the United States, in the early 80's, Nancy Reagan spearheaded the famous Just-Say-No crusade which was allied to her husband's declared war on drugs.

However, with the benefit of hindsight, it is generally acknowledged that neither of these anti-drugs campaigns achieved any lasting impact, and for the duration of the campaigns drug use actually increased. Both are now commonly cited as examples of how not to run an anti-drugs campaign.

So how should the issue of drugs be tackled? Are high-profile anti-drugs campaigns the right way to go about it?

By their very nature anti-drugs campaigns tend to be reactive; some are conceived and launched on the back of a dramatic event, often involving a high-profile drug-related death. The result is often an emotive campaign involving bereaved relatives and publicity-seeking politicians rather than a carefully prepared and reasoned response which identifies where the problems are and how to tackle them.

For too long now politicians have used the issue of drugs as some sort of political football which they assume, if kicked hard enough, will convince the electorate that they are tough on law and order. Not surprisingly, nothing constructive ever gets done that way. What usually happens next is that, after an initial burst of media interest, whatever anti-drugs campaign has been instigated eventually fades away with no lasting results. Until the next high-profile tragedy comes along when the whole thing starts up all over again. Clearly this isn't the most effective way to tackle a complex issue like drug use.

One of the most recent anti-drugs campaigns, *Scotland Against Drugs*, is a good example of the above, and as it embraces the current political thinking on drug policy, *SAD* needs to be analysed to see what lessons can be learned for the future. It's fair to say that those who aren't prepared to learn from the mistakes of the past are doomed to repeat them.

THE THINKING BEHIND *SAD*

The current political climate in Scotland – like most other Western countries – is one where for many years now there has been a deafening silence on the subject of spending public money on things like jobs, houses, education or health. It's a sad state of affairs but that's the way it is. However, silence doesn't last long in politics. There's only one thing you can do with silence and that's fill it with noise. So with a general election looming, what a perfect opportunity it was for an opportunist politician to pick up a large law-and-order drum and beat it for all it was worth.

Enter Michael Forsyth MP, then Secretary of State for Scotland, and his all-new, all-singing, all-dancing (yes, it came to that), anti-drugs crusade: *Scotland Against Drugs (SAD)*.

The timing of the launch of *SAD* could not have been more

opportunistic on the part of Mr Forsyth. The tabloid press had been going hysterical about drugs following the death of a young girl, Leah Betts, in the south of England – who had (supposedly) died from the effects of taking the dance drug ecstasy. Closer to home, three young men had died in 1995 after attending an Ayrshire club – Hanger 13 – again, supposedly from the effects of taking ecstasy. Combined with fears over drug-related crime and the record number of drug deaths in Scotland – 102 people had died in 1995 from heroin and methadone overdoses in the Strathclyde area alone[6] – the moral climate was ripe for exploiting.

And what better time for a government to initiate an anti-drugs campaign than in the run-up to a general election which from a Conservative point of view was looking increasingly unwinable.

The way the campaign was launched was as lamentable as it was predictable. Instead of a reasoned analysis and extensive survey of why people use drugs, before going on to discover which drugs are being used, which drugs are causing problems, and thereby drawing some practical conclusions on how to help both drug users and the communities they live in, this is how Michael Forsyth introduced the *Scotland Against Drugs* campaign:

> "Once again our way of life is threatened, this time by an enemy within. The drugs epidemic is a scourge as terrible as any mediaeval plague. Let us, as a nation, make a New Year resolution that 1996 is the year in which we will turn back the tide of drug abuse which is engulfing our young people and threatening our civilisation. Our aim is nothing less than to win back Scotland from the drug culture and liberate a generation."[7]

We should have seen it coming. History has taught us time and time again that official anti-drug campaigns always begin by demonising drugs and drug users.

This time, though, the Secretary of State for Scotland went much farther. Not content with describing drugs as a "mediaeval plague" he had gone on to describe drug users as the new "enemy within".

It was easy to see where Forsyth was coming from. It's an absolute of political life that faltering economies need scapegoats. That's the insidious way in which reactionary politicians have always operated. The unfortunate aspect of this was that the other political leaders in Scotland, despite any private reservations they might have held, let Forsyth get away with this ill-conceived initiative for fear they would be seen as being soft on law and order in a pre-election period.

In the wake of Forsyth's speech, however, alarm bells were ringing across the country. The possibility of a state-led drug war was not one to be relished. Not surprisingly drug workers were horrified at the prospect. Organisations like Crew 2000 in Edinburgh, Aberdeen Drug Action, Enhance in Glasgow, and many others had been quietly and effectively working with and gaining the confidence and trust of young drug users – without being judgmental – yet here was officialdom planning a full-scale assault on drug users and drug culture which could seriously jeopardise their work.

Thankfully, in the words of Burns, Scotland's national poet, *"the best laid schemes o' mice and men gang aft agley."* Which in the case of Forsyth and his plans for the *SAD* campaign, roughly translated meant, the public quickly smelt a rat.

A behind-the-scenes rethink was done and pretty quickly a new look *Scotland Against Drugs* was unveiled with Michael Forsyth unceremoniously removed from centre-stage and a new user-friendly interface in the form of David Macauley was installed as the £40,000-a-year Campaign Director. And since the *SAD* campaign was initially intended to be nothing more than a quick political fix then who better to preside over it than Mr. Kwik Fit himself, Tom Farmer.

Closer examination, however, revealed the real reasons behind the launch and timing of *SAD*. The campaign was devised to replace the work of other bodies whose findings were not in tune with the thinking of the (then) Conservative government.

The roots of *SAD* go back to May 1994 when an all-party Commons Scottish Select Committee investigation into drug abuse in Scotland came up with a series of recommendations to tackle what they saw was a real and growing problem. They recommended such ideas as increasing the use of methadone to treat heroin addicts; setting up local drug liaison committees to identify the extent of drug misuse in rural Scotland; establishing drug crisis centres in Glasgow and Edinburgh; and the introduction of fiscal fines for minor cannabis offences.

The *SAD* committee, which would now co-ordinate the fight against drugs in Scotland also effectively replaced the role of another previous organisation – the much-vaunted Ministerial Drugs Task Force – whose 102-page report *Drugs In Scotland: Meeting The Challenge*, published in October '94, made a number of well-researched, carefully-chosen recommendations not dissimilar to those of the Select Committee's. This report was published just a few months after the Committee's recommendations and concluded starkly that "the root causes of the worst of Scotland's drug problems are to be found in a deadly combination of a youth culture which endorses drug-taking, and multiple deprivation."

This wasn't a conclusion that Michael Forsyth would have wanted to hear. Especially all that nonsense about "multiple deprivation" and spending public money on services. Going softer on cannabis users was hardly a vote-winner either. Forsyth and his appointees decided that *SAD* wouldn't tie its hands behind its back with such ideological baggage. A strong anti-drugs message wedded to tough police enforcement would be their key to success.

Cutting across what had gone before, Forsyth then delivered his apocalyptic New Year's speech and announced that the war against drugs had begun in earnest. He trumpeted loudly the founding of *Scotland Against Drugs*, a crusade "to encourage people to resist and reject the use of drugs."

There was no talk at this stage of consultation with existing drug agencies, nor developing the successfully pioneered harm reduction measures, nor public resources being made available for detox centres, more drugs workers, or suchlike. It was intended to be a blatant and unequivocal Just-Say-No initiative allied to a law enforcement crack down.

Two weeks after his announcement, Forsyth convened a meeting of churchmen, political leaders, media sorts, police, health officials and a few hand-picked drug workers to discuss the setting up of *Scotland Against Drugs*. Wary, after the hammering his New Year speech received, he adopted a more even-handed approach. Those present agreed to support the initiative.

However, Forsyth still saw the whole venture as a publicity vehicle for himself and at the second meeting of *SAD*, in London, proposed himself as chairman ie public mouthpiece of the campaign. Unsurprisingly, this was vigorously opposed and Forsyth had to eat humble pie when Tom Farmer was proposed and was adopted instead.

A launch date was set first for March 18th and then, because of the tragedy at Dunblane, put back to May 7th 1996 when *Scotland Against Drugs* was duly launched in a carefully orchestrated blaze of publicity.

Support for *SAD* was by no means universal. Many foresaw not only a huge waste of public money but the dangers of an opportunist campaign by politicians which would only fuel the prevailing anti-drugs hysteria. On the day that *SAD* was launched with a national tour of Scottish cities, an alternative press conference was convened by myself and others in Glasgow to launch *Scotland Against Drugs Hypocrisy* (*SADH*).

SADH was supported at its launch by: Dr. John Marks, an eminent clinical psychiatrist in Merseyside who had pioneered the prescription of pharmaceutical heroin to addicts; Claire Wyburn, the Dance Editor of M8 music magazine; Graeme Steel, son of former Liberal Party leader David Steel and a cannabis activist who had been sentenced to jail for 9 months for growing the drug; Tommy Sheridan, the Militant Glasgow Councillor who went to jail for his political stance against the Poll Tax; as well as support from Linda Hendry of the Green Party and author Irvine Welsh. The purpose of the *SADH* launch was to try and cut across the idea that the whole nation was united in a war against drugs and to show that there were a lot of people out there who did not want to see yet another futile Just-Say-No campaign.

To an extent, *SADH* worked effectively at the time, sharing equal billing on the national news that night and in the next days papers. We succeeded in letting it be known that there was serious opposition to what we saw as the ill-conceived objectives of *SAD*. We asked how could this be an anti-drugs campaign if it ignored alcohol and tobacco since they were the two most dangerous drugs in society – killing an estimated 160,000 people every year between them?[8] And we asked why they were lumping all illegal drugs together rather than identifying the ones which were causing a problem? Neither of these questions were answered by representatives of *SAD* at the time. They still haven't been.

SO WHAT WERE THE AIMS OF
SCOTLAND AGAINST DRUGS?

Michael Forsyth seemed to be clear: *"Within the umbrella of* Scotland Against Drugs *there will be an opportunity for people to take all sorts of approaches, provided their principal objective is to get people to turn against drugs and to bring the evil men and woman who are drugs pushers to justice."* [9] In other words Just-Say-No plus Law Enforcement.

David Macauley, the *SAD* Campaign Director, stated that the campaign: *"would have to have originality rather than send the same old stereotypical messages. This is going to have to be cleverer and more effective."* Not different in substance, just "cleverer." He too reiterated from the outset that *"a vital part of the £1 million campaign is to persuade young people that drug-taking is morally and socially wrong."* [10]

A 35-strong advisory council to *SAD* was announced on 6th May 96. The make-up of the committee again suggested the likely direction the campaign would take.

Members of the media (10), politicians (8), business community (4), social work, education and health board officials (4), celebrities (2), church (2) and police (1) accounted for no less than 31 positions on the *SAD* advisory council.

Instead of pulling together a committee of individuals who had a wide range of experience in working with drug users *SAD* opted for a committee loaded with opinion formers. Most of these 31 hand-picked individuals had no more experience in dealing with day-to-day drug problems than anyone you might pass in the street. It could be deduced from the backgrounds of this pick-and-mix assortment of individuals that this was going to be a propaganda-led campaign from Day One.

Two of the remaining places on the committee were given to the chairs of the Glasgow Drug Action Team and Scottish Drug Forum and a further two places were given to individuals who worked on a day-to-day basis with drug users: David Bryce from Calton Athletic Drug Rehabilitation Group and consultant psychiatrist Dr Judy Greenwood.

Drug advice organisations like Crew 2000 and Enhance, who successfully operate harm reduction programmes, and importantly, have the trust of thousands of young drug users, were excluded from the advisory body.

At this stage, *SAD* didn't seem to realise that young people they were hoping to reach were part of a generation which had a greater understanding of drugs and drug culture than any previous generation. This generation was all too aware that while it was a criminal offence to use illegal drugs like cannabis or ecstasy – more dangerous drugs such as alcohol and tobacco were legally on sale.

How could a campaign against illicit drugs be justified when it ignores a legal drug like alcohol which is implicated in 60 per cent of suicides, 40 per cent of acts of domestic violence, 20 per cent of child abuse cases, nearly one third of drownings and 39 per cent of domestic fires?[11] Unless the basic hypocrisy of *SAD*'s position was addressed – of only being against ILLEGAL drugs – then much of the campaign's message was going to fall on deaf ears.

One appointee to the *SAD* committee showed just how deep this hypocritical approach to legal drugs went. Jim Faulds of Faulds Advertising was appointed as one of the 35 *SAD* advisory committee members. His chief responsibility would be the advertising campaign which would be a main component of the *SAD* crusade. However, as well as directing *SAD*'s propaganda against drug use, Faulds Advertising is also responsible for some other notable clients. Such as Glenmorangie, Black Bottle Whisky, Gloag's Gin, Macallan-Glenlivet and Scottish Courage, which includes the McEwans's Ale range. Could this be the same company which is responsible for splashing the words McEwan's Lager across Glasgow Rangers football shirts which are then sold to young kids all over Scotland? Far from being anti-drugs this hypocritical company actively promotes drugs!

A MEDIA-LED CAMPAIGN

And so the *SAD* campaign began on 7th May 1996 with a start that most of them would rather forget. Michael Forsyth and the other three political leaders set forth in a *SAD* battle bus, donned a sweatshirt over their shirts and ties, turned their baseball hats back-to-front, went techno-dancing at an afternoon "rave", and were met with immediate laughter and ridicule. After this PR disaster, David Macauley took over the publicity reins.

SAD's strategy soon became apparent. After initial talk about the need for community involvement and a variety of approaches including harm reduction, it was decided that the bulk of the million pounds (£900,000 of it)[12] was to be poured into a year-long, glossy, high-profile, advertising campaign. (A second fund became available to *SAD* later in the year – the Challenge Fund – which had in its coffers £531,000 which came from both the Scottish Office and from the business community.)

Despite a publicly stated commitment to harm reduction policies, only one solitary grant of £27,500 to Enhance in Glasgow – out of a total of £1,531,000 – went to harm reduction projects.

To go down the road of a national advertising campaign was all the more surprising considering David Macauley had gone on record as stating:

> *"Education on its own has been proved time and time again to be ineffective. You can't educate a kid to death. If you don't give him something useful to do with his time and he lives in an area where drugs are endemic, all the education in the world will not protect him."* [13]

Critics of *SAD*'s strategy soon began to surface.

Brian Cavanagh, Edinburgh's Social Work boss was one who attacked *SAD*'s message:

> *"Just-Say-No is a facile response to drugs – it's not good enough. We need to be realistic and honest and realise that drugs are here to stay, and let's find the best way of educating people."* [14]

Many others who worked in the drug field were privately critical of *SAD* but were afraid to say anything because of funding considerations.

Just a few weeks before the *SAD* advertising campaign was launched, and in a bizarre duplication of resources, the *Health Education Board for Scotland* (*HEBS*) produced three ads entitled *Ecstasy*, *Acid* and *Speed* which ran on TV and cinemas from October of that year. These weren't much different in style or content from the *SAD* ads and were an indication at the lack of co-ordination between *SAD* and the existing health education bodies. These ads were aimed at 15-19 year olds who had experience of drug use and showed images of snakes crawling out of strawberries, doves suffering fits in mid-flight, and egg-timers exploding (ie you're running out of time kids). The ads were narrated by film star Ewan McGregor – apparently "because he is a credible actor rather than because he was in *Trainspotting*".[15] Aye, right.

Geoff Young, chairman of the community-based liaison committee set up by Scottish Drugs Forum, was quick to point out after seeing the ads that they "marked a return to the criticised

Just-Say-No anti-drugs campaign of the 1980s" and that "the message would not be seen as credible by young people."[16]

Undeterred, the *SAD* advertising campaign duly followed.

The first introductory wave of these ads went out in newspapers, billboards and flyers and were aimed at making parents aware of the extent of drug use around them.

Then came the second and main phase of the *SAD* advertisements. These were produced for television and radio and were backed up with billboard posters and magazine flyers aimed at a young, mainly teenage audience.

SAD claimed that these ads were produced as the result of their own "research" among young people. Macauley explained the thinking behind the ads:

> "*We are not trying to preach or to tell them not to take drugs, because that approach simply does not work. This campaign has been thoroughly researched right through to the language and terminology used and we hope ... they will take in the message.*"[17]

And the ads themselves which were to use up the lion's share of the *SAD* funding?

They were set around the dance scene and concentrated on the use of dance drugs such as ecstasy, acid and speed – although only ecstasy was actually named. The world portrayed in the ads was virtually unrecognisable for the majority of young people. It was a world where dance drugs were cut with rat poison; where a guy takes a helpless young girl back to his flat and tries to rape her; where a young girl wakes up in bed with a 'mysterious attractive stranger' and can't remember what she has done because she has taken ecstasy; where a dealer sells 'rubbish' to strangers; claims that "hundreds of Scots died from drugs last year"; and claims that ecstasy, acid, and speed cause among other things spots and rotten teeth. There was even a scene in one ad where a doctor does a post-mortem on a corpse explaining the harm ecstasy does to the lungs.

The ads didn't actually TELL anyone not to take drugs but instead they opted to SHOW the dangers of taking these drugs in order to SCARE young people into just saying no. What we got as a result was a subtle change of emphasis, away from old-fashioned preaching, true, but still no change in the actual substance or intended objective.

Unfortunately for *SAD*, the information presented in the ads ranged from the inaccurate to the completely untrue. They were a crude lesson in misinformation and disinformation and ended up with little credibility among the target audience.

Here are a few examples:

1. *Drugs are cut with rat poison.*
This claim was based on a Strathclyde Police report from the early 1980s when a drug called Warfarin was reputedly cut with heroin. (Incidentally, at no point is heroin mentioned in any of the ads – a case of misplaced priorities if ever there was one). Although, it is true that Warfarin *is* used as a rat poison it is also widely available to humans on prescription: to thin blood after a heart bypass. There is no record of any dance drugs in the '90s being cut with rat poison.

2. *Ecstasy makes women helpless and easy prey for rapists.*
In actual fact helplessness is not a feeling associated with ecstasy use. In many cases women feel empowered and more confident on ecstasy. This may be due to the fact that the culture that has developed around the ecstasy/dance scene is one where women feel safe to dress any way they want without guys molesting or manhandling them in the way that would more likely happen

down the alcohol-fueled pubs and discos. Helplessness is much more associated with the drug alcohol than illegal dance drugs.

3. *Ecstasy leads to memory loss.*
Again not true. Ecstasy users tend to remember everything from the night before, often vividly. Memory loss is again something more readily associated primarily with alcohol abuse.

4. *Dealers in clubs sell rubbish to strangers.*
Most people buy their ecstasy from people they know. Most dealers use the ecstasy they sell themselves and want their customers to have a good time and come back again. There's just no financial incentive for a dealer to sell rubbish as their name would soon become mud and the customers wouldn't come back.

5. *Ecstasy causes lung damage.*
While the jury is still out with regards to the long-term effect of ecstasy on the brain's serotonin levels, medical experts have concluded that it is not responsible for lung damage. I'm tempted to speculate that the *SAD* ads have got ecstasy mixed up with the legal drug tobacco.

6. *Hundreds of Scots died from drugs last year.*
The actual figure in 1995 was 251.[18] Of those, 155 were known or suspected to be from taking habit forming drugs such as heroin and methadone. The remaining 96 drug deaths included suicides using legal painkillers such as paracetemol. In the eyes of many young drug users, the ads again failed to put these drug deaths into perspective by comparing them to the 20,000 Scots who die annually from tobacco-related illnesses and the estimated 4,000 Scots who die each year from alcohol-related illnesses. Predictably, legal drugs such as alcohol, tobacco and tranquillisers weren't mentioned in

the *SAD* campaign. More surprisingly, nor was heroin, which most people consider to be the illicit drug causing the most problems. When you consider the cumulative health and social problems created by the use of alcohol, tobacco, tranquillisers and heroin, then the three dance drugs that *SAD* specifically chose to attack in their first year – ecstasy, LSD and speed – seem almost benign in comparison.

7. *Dance drugs cause things like spots and rotten teeth.*
When you consider the effect on Scotland's health that malnutrition, poverty, and poor diets have, then this "warning" about the problems associated with illegal drugs comes over as a bit spurious to say the least.

There were two basic problems with the *SAD* advertising campaign which, unfortunately, tend to be common to almost every anti-drugs campaign.

Firstly; as shown above, the basic information going out to the targeted audience is seen as being neither credible nor accurate. Young people aren't stupid. Experienced drug worker Max Cruickshank, who wrote the information book used by the National Drugs Helpline, put it in a nutshell: *"Teenagers have antennae like nobody's business. So there's a real danger in portraying something that's exceedingly rare – if it even exists at all – as normal. You must give kids the plain facts. If they find out you're talking crap, they'll reject your whole message."* [19]

The second problem with these ads is that the central message consists of trying to warn people about the dangers of taking drugs by using scare stories and shock tactics. Unfortunately, more times than not, this has the opposite effect. It's almost like laying down a dare or a challenge. This was the opinion of the Scottish Drugs Forum, who, in a leaked memo published in *The*

Big Issue Scotland, alerted fellow *SAD* members to the danger of this approach: *"Shock-horror approaches have been evaluated in the context of school drug education programmes and have been shown to lead to increased experimentation within the target group. The concern is therefore that mass media campaigns of a hard-hitting shock-horror nature do not lead to the desired change in behaviour, but can often achieve the opposite."* [20]

A SECOND *SAD* YEAR

Despite a clamour of reservations about the direction *SAD* had chosen to go, a further £2 million was allocated to *SAD* for the next financial year. This was a year which saw a change of government.

SAD planned to kick off Year Two with yet another advertising campaign – this time in the shape of a Drugs Awareness Week beginning on June 23rd 97 – Faulds Advertising prepared the new ads. Some 218 billboard posters carried the message:

WHAT DO YOU CALL KIDS WHO TAKE DRUGS?
A. THE MAJORITY.
56% OF 16 YEAR OLDS HAVE TAKEN ILLEGAL DRUGS.

To say this message was ambiguous is an understatement. Any young person reading that would probably have interpreted this as a green light to take drugs if they hadn't already started. The billboard was saying it was the norm.

Two other billboard ads had even more insidious messages. One stately simply:

THE HEALTH SERVICE HAS OD'd ON DRUG USERS.
DRUG-RELATED HOSPITAL ADMISSIONS ARE UP
TENFOLD SINCE 1980.

Another ad stated:

MANY DRUG USERS TAKE HEROIN, SPEED AND VCR's.
70% OF ALL THEFTS ARE DRUG-RELATED.

There was no useful information. No explanation. The *SAD* campaign had turned full circle and had gone back to Michael Forsyth's original message of smearing drug users as a plague in our midst who were to be vilified for wasting public resources and thieves who would break in to your house and rob you. While this may be the case for the very small percentage of drug users who are addicted to drugs like heroin, for the majority of recreational drug users this was an unsubstantiated slur and a downright lie. It was fanning the public's fear of drug users unnecessarily.

It comes back to hypocrisy too. If the *SAD* people had gone into any hospital casualty ward on a Friday or Saturday night they would have found that the main drug which has filled up the waiting room was alcohol. Similarly, the drug which causes the biggest drain on health service resources is tobacco, responsible for around 100,000 deaths in the UK every year. So why no mention of these drugs? *SAD* had yet again made the fundamental mistake of lumping all illegal drugs under one banner. These ads were either deliberately misleading or just plain ignorant. Either way, they did nothing to further anyone's understanding of drug use.

However the impact of these ads at the beginning of *SAD*'s Drugs Awareness Week was marginalised by a tragic event a few days earlier. An event which would prove that *SAD* had no real direction but merely reacted to events, making up policy on the hoof. It would also be the event which would throw the whole *SAD* campaign into bitter recriminations.

On June 19th the life-support system of a 13-year-old Lanarkshire boy, Andrew Woodlock, was switched off. He had taken three tablets of ecstasy in the woods near his home. A friend had taken five of the same pills. Andrew had panicked as the drugs kicked in and drank too much water thinking it would counter the effects of the ecstasy. Just like Leah Betts before him his brain had become fatally damaged from water poisoning.

Confronted with an understandably grief-stricken mother, David Macauley blamed Andrew's death on the harm reduction advice projects for "peddling the myth that drugs could be taken safely" suggesting something "needed to be done about them."[21]

In one fell stroke all the good work that had been done over a period of years gaining the trust of young drug users was undermined and hard-working experienced drug workers were ignorantly called *"pro-drug"* and *"happy-clappy, middle-class muesli eaters"* [22] by the likes of *SAD*'s media advisor Jack Irvine.

In response, drug workers, the more intelligent leader writers, and even members of *SAD*'s own advisory committee hit back. Chief Constable of Lothian and Borders Police, Roy Cameron, a *SAD* member and chair of the Association of Chief Police Officers in Scotland, stated that the campaign was no longer useful and critisised Macauley for his attacks on harm reduction. Nine members of the Scottish Advisory Committee on Drug Misuse, experts who help the Scottish Office draw up drug policy, wrote to Donald Dewar, the new Scottish Secretary warning: *"It is our belief that SAD has been, to say the least, unhelpful in assisting the development of an effective response to drug use in Scotland".* [23] These nine included another *SAD* committee member, Dr Judy Greenwood.

In the public's eyes there was an open battle between supporters of harm reduction and those of the Just-Say-No approach. And then just as things couldn't get any more volatile, David Macauley dragged the poor mother of the dead boy onto a public platform to support his attack on harm reduction projects. A move which was cynically calculated to provoke the tabloids into a frenzy of emotional manipulation in the aftermath of the tragedy. And of course the tabloids duly did their worst. The result was chaos, confusion and a complete loss of credibility for *SAD*.

LEARNING FROM PREVIOUS MISTAKES

It is likely that *SAD* will go the way of previous anti-drugs campaigns and be wound up. *SAD* has done nothing but damage to the important work being done by people who have genuine experience in the drugs field. But more importantly, when the dust has settled from the *Scotland Against Drugs* fiasco, it would be useful if whatever or whoever comes next – Tony Blair's 'drugs tsar' included – were to ensure that *SAD*'s mistakes are not repeated.

Chief among the mistakes to be avoided is the exclusion of legal drugs like alcohol and tobacco from the equation. Given the damage these drugs cause both socially and in terms of health, *SAD* was justifiably seen in the eyes of many young people as being a hypocritical campaign from day one.

Drug education cannot be based on worse-case scenarios with misleading or inaccurate information. Young people will switch off if the information doesn't tally up with their own experiences.

But most importantly of all, it has to be understood that expensive high-profile anti-drugs campaigns carried out in the media just *do not work*. In the *SAD*-sponsored survey published in the run up to their Drugs Awareness Week it was found that only 4 per cent of young people are likely to listen to the media when thinking about illegal drugs.[24] Maybe *SAD* should have commissioned this survey *before* they wasted £900,000 of public money on media advertising; money which could have been better spent investing in drug support workers on the ground. Unfortunately they haven't learned from this. In October '97, *SAD* announced the launch of yet another high-profile – and no doubt just as expensive – advertising campaign planned for the media.

High-profile anti-drug campaigns actually achieve the opposite from what they intend. They increase curiosity about drugs which can lead to an increase in their use. Telling young people not to take drugs, or trying to scare them off drugs by exaggerating the dangers, simply adds to the allure, excitement and glamour of doing something illegal.

While there is definitely a burning need for honest and accurate drug education among school children and young people there is just as definitely NO PLACE WHATSOEVER for national media-led campaigns. They only make things worse.

The rest of this book argues that a new approach needs to be adopted. A fundamentally different approach from that taken by *Scotland Against Drugs*. A new approach which recognises the mistakes of the past and which faces up to recreational drug use honestly and without preconceived notions of what is right and what is wrong. This means being flexible, pragmatic, and courageous enough to take whatever difficult or controversial decisions are necessary.

A NEW APPROACH BASED ON HARM REDUCTION

Existing drug policies have been based on the idea that drug use is a bad thing and that it can be stamped out, or at least curtailed, through tougher law enforcement measures and educating young people into saying no to drugs. It is a strategy that is rarely questioned by government policy makers. The only flaw in this seemingly obvious strategy is that existing drug policies have been responsible for a continual rise in the number of people taking illegal drugs, a continual rise in drug-related offences, and a continual rise in the number of drug addicts and drug-related deaths.

There is an old saying that if ain't broke don't fix it. It follows that the reverse must also be the case.

WHO IS USING DRUGS?

Any number of surveys have been carried out to determine who is using what drugs. The results of these surveys vary according to the methods used and the type of results anticipated by those who word and commission them. These are the results of two such surveys, one published in the *Independent on Sunday* and one published in *Scotland on Sunday* and commissioned by *SAD*.

A look at the results of the Scottish survey should leave nobody in any doubt as to the scale of drug use. A third of all adults in

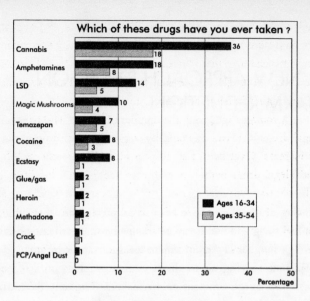

CHART 1 (Ind on Sun, 28/1/96)[1]

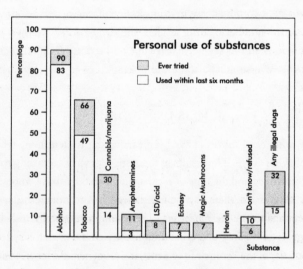

CHART 2 (Scot On Sun, 22/6/97)[2]

Scotland (32 per cent) have taken illegal drugs – 15 per cent of them in the last six months. This is broadly in line with the national survey which found that 34 per cent of adults aged 16-34 have taken cannabis – although it is generally acknowledged that drug use is slightly higher in Scotland than in the rest of the UK.

For a younger age group the number of people who have taken illegal drugs increases dramatically suggesting that drug use is on the increase. Over half of all 16 year olds (53 per cent) will have tried illegal drugs before they leave school.[3] More localised, but still extensive, surveys carried out by Crew 2000 found that 73 per cent of 16-30 year olds in Glasgow had used illegal drugs.[4] Another survey found that 67 per cent of young people – average age 19 – had used illegal drugs within the last six months.[5]

Whatever way you want to interpret these surveys one thing is clear. These are not inconsiderable numbers. Therefore, a realistic approach to drugs begins with accepting that illegal drug use is here to stay for the foreseeable future whether we like it or not. It is irrelevant whether anyone considers drug use to be an evil in our midst or the best thing since sliced bread. People will continue to use drugs regardless. The choice facing our society is that we can either shun drug users, vilify them, criminalise them and expend a fortune on trying to stop them OR we can accept that since drug use is going to continue anyway we should try and reduce whatever harm it might cause.

WHY DO PEOPLE USE DRUGS?

This should really be the first question that anyone wanting to understand drug use should ask. There are no simple answers like "to get high". The reasons for drug use are complex and vary from person to person, from drug to drug, and from occasion to occasion. If you think of all the different reasons why people take alcohol, for instance, you would start to get an idea of the variety of answers. It is time that a major study into this question was funded so that parents, in particular, can understand more about this one. It may lessen their fears and help them understand their children more.

It could take a whole book in itself to even scratch the surface of this question – and it would be a worthwhile book too. There would seem to be a strong need or desire within most people to alter their state of consciousness from time to time. Even if it's just a couple of glasses of sherry at New Year to help get in the party mood. (What else is that but altering one's state of mind or consciousness with the aid of a recreational drug?)

Instead of going into an academic treatise on the psychology of the mind, I've reprinted the results of a survey carried out among 976 young people – two thirds of whom had used illegal drugs. They gave their reasons why they took them.

REASONS GIVEN FOR USING DRUGS[6]

Reasons given:	No.	%
Pleasure and enjoyment: For the buzz	353	46%
Sociability: Relax with friends	155	20%
Negative life circumstances: Escape from problems	83	11%
Peer pressure: All my friends do	52	7%
Experimentation: To see what it was like	35	5%
Anti-alcohol: Better than drinking	29	4%
Don't know: Never thought about it	26	3%
Other: Because illegal	15	2%
Physical circumstances: Due to operation	10	1%
Problem usage: I need them	10	1%
Total	**768**	**100%**

Rather than commenting, I'll leave it for readers to mull over the answers. Suffice to note that problem drug-taking was pretty low overall which would bear out the theory that most people who use illegal drugs don't have a problem them. Much more research of this nature needs to be done.

HARM REDUCTION

In the aftermath of the death of 13 year old Andrew Woodlock, a number of drug projects took some over-the-top criticism for providing harm reduction advice. David Macauley of *SAD* said: "Something has to be done about those groups who receive public money and then try to peddle the myth that drugs can be taken safely."[7] Macauley's allies within *SAD*: Jack Irvine, his media advisor, and David Bryce, founder of Calton Athletic, supported him. Bryce has gone on record as saying "there is no safe way to take drugs."[8] And in some respects he's right. There isn't. All drugs carry some sort of risk no matter how small. (Bryce's organisation use football to help build a team spirit among the ex-addicts he works with. It's a successful approach – for some – and one that deserves public backing. But in reality, there's no safe way to play football either.)

None of these individuals had the courage to criticise the work of any specific organisation although it was clear that their criticisms were directed at the likes of Crew 2000 and Enhance who give valuable harm reduction advice. Macauley wrote at the time: *"Many of these harm reduction groups are almost promoting what they would class as safe drugs use."* [9]

I would challenge Macauley, or any of the other harm reduction critics to find *one* piece of information that has ever been produced by any of these organisations – leaflet or otherwise – which states how to take drugs safely. They won't – because there isn't any.

This is one of the great myths peddled by those who should know better.

For example, Crew 2000 put out a leaflet called 'Smack Attack' which was aimed at heroin users and those considering using heroin. It took a lot of stick at the time being accused of encouraging heroin use. Yet nowhere on the leaflet does it use the word *safe*. Just like all the harm reduction advice it is the word *safer* that is used. *Safer* injecting, *safer* smoking. There is a world of difference.

Crew 2000 also put out a leaflet entitled 'If You Use Ecstasy'. It advised:

> "If you're NOT dancing or you're taking E at home you won't need to drink as much water. There have been a few RARE cases of people dying from drinking too much water when they're not dancing which results in the body retaining excess fluid and the blood becoming diluted. SO – only drink enough water to quench your thirst."

Sadly, Andrew Woodlock and Leah Betts were two of those rare cases who died as a result of drinking too much water because they thought it was the right thing to do. And here is the tragedy of it all. If they and their friends had been aware of such non-judgmental factual information they might both be alive today. How could anyone in their right mind criticise such potentially life-saving information going out to young people?

WHO IS BEST QUALIFIED TO GIVE DRUG ADVICE?

Non-judgmental harm reduction organisations are the way forward. They don't preach abstinence, they don't criticise drug users, nor do they say that drug use is okay. They just give facts and advice in a way that young people can relate to.

Who actually gives the advice is important. If it is going to be done in schools, for example, it has to come from people that schoolchildren can relate to. There's no point using authority figures like the police or teachers. Most young people in secondary schools will just yawn and ignore them. This was borne out by SAD's own survey.[10] They asked which audiences young people were likely to listen to when thinking about illegal drugs. Only 5 per cent said the police. An even smaller 4 per cent said the media. Teachers came in at 10 per cent but it was other young people who scored highest at 37 per cent. Another survey found that only 2 per cent of young people surveyed in Edinburgh thought that the media gave good advice on drugs with 17 per cent thinking the media gave bad advice.[11]

Drug education is important. It can save lives and reduce the harm that drugs can cause. But who actually gives the advice can be decisive on whether it is heeded or not. If you ask young people they will tell you that they *do* want advice on drugs but it has to be advice from people who know what they are talking about, people who have used drugs themselves, people who know what pitfalls to avoid, and who won't exaggerate the dangers. Teachers, the police, and other authority figures have virtually no constructive role to play in this because their information is second hand (mostly); young people will feel inhibited from discussing their own drug experiences; and those who are most likely to use drugs will ignore them simply because they are authority figures.

The volunteers and workers at Crew 2000 and Enhance are comprised mainly from young people who have used drugs before and know what they are talking about. *These* are the people who should be going round the schools and youth clubs. Other young people will listen attentively and talk openly about their own experiences when they are confident they won't get reported for what they've done.

The preparedness for both young people and parents to consult non-judgmental harm reduction groups was proven by the success of the premises opened up by Enhance in Glasgow. Between November '96 and March '97 Enhance estimated that 8,500 people visited their shop front in the city centre. Mainly young people wanting information on drugs but also a fair number of concerned parents. 800 questionnaires were distributed and it became evident that around 70 per cent of those coming into the shop had taken illicit drugs. In less than five months, Enhance printed and distributed 12,000 copies of their newsletter *Gibberish* and in total 45,000 information units such as advice leaflets were distributed from the shop. These weren't unsolicited leaflets dropping through letterboxes but leaflets and booklets which were specifically sought after and read. There was no waste.

With sufficient funding, premises like these should have been set up in every city and in every town in the country. The ambience of the premises, with DJs playing, and a relaxed informal atmosphere, would ensure that they attracted the very people that such information needs to reach. Unfortunately, Enhance's city centre premises were closed down in March '97 through lack of funding and another opportunity was wasted as millions were ploughed elsewhere into SAD's futile advertising campaigns.

HARM REDUCTION IS ABOUT MORE THAN JUST GIVING ADVICE

Harm reduction has become the drug buzzword of the nineties. It has been embraced by both anti-drug campaigners and prohibitionist politicians, as well as those drug workers who give non-judgemental advice to users. When David Macauley of *Scotland Against Drugs* claimed to be in favour of harm reduction – he supported a grant of £27,500 to Enhance and supported the methadone maintenance programme for heroin addicts – he unwittingly highlighted part of the confusion the term causes. When the other David Macauley of *Scotland Against Drugs* attacked those harm reduction organisations who "peddle the myth that drugs can be taken safely" he seemed to even confuse himself.

Harm Reduction is not the same as Some Harm Reduction. You can't pick and choose which drug users you want to help. Harm reduction means reducing as much of the harm associated with drug use as is humanly possible. This doesn't just mean advice or education on safer drug practices, but also means providing the facilities and support necessary to help all drug users, as well as tackling the harm that the illegal status of drugs causes for both drug users and the wider community they live in. Furthermore, it means devising an approach which aims to reduce the harm associated with legal drugs such as alcohol, tobacco and tranquillisers. It's no use explaining the risks of taking ecstasy honestly and clearly if cigarette and alcohol manufacturers are allowed to promote their drugs on every hoarding and magazine page they can buy. Promotion of any drugs – legal or illegal – is unacceptable.

Most important of all, though, if harm reduction is really to be worthy of the name it also means taking political measures to tackle unemployment, bad housing, low wages, lack of decent sport and leisure facilities, and a general lack of opportunities for young people. These are underlying factors for a lot of problem drug use. All of these factors have to be addressed if the amount of harm that drugs do is to be reduced.

NO MORE LUMPING ALL DRUGS TOGETHER

At present you would think that there are only two types of

drugs – legal and illegal. (The legal ones are okay but the illegal ones are dangerous substances that need to be eradicated. This simplistic approach is still the official thinking on the subject.) A more practical approach would be to look at each drug or category of drug *individually*. To equate heroin with ecstasy is patently ridiculous but in the eyes of the law they are both categorised as equally dangerous Class A substances. Similarly, alcohol and tobacco have only minimal differences in legal age limits yet both carry different degrees of health risk – and both are much more addictive and life-threatening than either cannabis or LSD for example. Generalised drug categories don't help.

The catch-all use of the word "drugs" to mean any substance the government decides to ban is part of the problem. It is important to identify which specific drugs are being referred to at all times. That way, when Government Minister George Robertson, says *"what we need is a single message about the evils of drugs"* [12] we know exactly which drugs he is talking about and whether he includes the legal drug alcohol which his parliamentary colleagues consume as they stagger between the fifteen bars of the House of Commons.

There are drugs – both legal and illegal – which *are* causing problems. There is an urgent need for both the drugs causing the problems, and the problems themselves, to be clearly identified. For example, if it is found that drugs such as alcohol, tobacco, tranquillisers, methadone and heroin are the ones causing the overwhelming bulk of health problems then these are the drugs which should be prioritised by government health campaigns.

DRUGS HYPOCRISY

It is probably too much to hope for but the debate on drugs needs some calm appraisal rather than hysterical headlines and pious condemnations. It would be helpful if the press took a break from using drugs to sell papers. Recently, for example, the Daily Mirror ran no less than nine different drug stories in one edition, including a front page lead and an editorial stating "We mustn't go soft on drug scum."[13] (This editorial might have made a sanctimonious leader-writer feel better with himself but it was just plain hypocrisy sitting beside the tobacco and alcohol ads.) What these publications don't even realise is that when they splatter drug horror stories across their pages they only increase drug curiosity and a desire to experiment. Far from warning people away from drugs they inadvertently lead to an increase in drug use because they glamorise drugs by making them out to be dangerous and risky. When Leah Betts died there were plenty of young clubbers who went out actually looking for the "apple" brand of ecstasy that she had taken. They had read about them in the papers and had seen the Sorted posters. The ads and publicity merely fuelled youthful bravado.

Hypocrisy with regards to legal drugs is a major concern for a lot of young people. For example, consider these well-publicised stories which illustrate the hypocritical way that all walks of society treat illegal and legal drug use.

When the Hibs striker Barry Lavety (then with St Mirren) was found to have taken an ecstasy on a night out clubbing with his mates a few years ago all hell broke loose. He was slammed for bringing the game of football into disrepute. He was sent for six weeks rehab to a drugs clinic in the countryside and not allowed any contact with the outside world. When he was eventually released from captivity he appeared suitably shamefaced and penitent and was forced to make anti-drug statements about the perils of drug abuse. And all this for taking one E. It was scarcely believable.

Then compare it with the treatment meted out to Glasgow Rangers superstar Ally McCoist. A person far more idolised by kids than Barry Lavety (in his St Mirren days), McCoist was caught drunk-driving by police after coming out of a night club in Glasgow when his car was seen swerving about in the middle of a main road. So what happens to the superstar whose stupidity under the influence of a mind-altering drug like alcohol put people's lives at risk ? He gets a driving ban, a paltry fine and a slap on the wrist from the judge. As far as Glasgow Rangers Football Club were concerned the matter was closed. And where was the media fury? Where was McCoist's embarrassed speech to a packed press conference on how he was sorry for bringing the game of football into disrepute? Where was the arm-up-the-back lecture to young people about the dangers of drink-driving? Nowhere. It was blatant hypocrisy and double-standards.

Similarly, when Hearts striker Stephane Paille was found with traces of a recreational drug in his blood he was sent home on the first jet back to France. This was for something he had done in his private life and nothing to do with his work. Yet when Paul Gascoigne downs a double whisky at half-time in a Celtic-Rangers match it's treated as a big joke. More hypocrisy.

When convicted cannabis smuggler Howard Marks was due to be released from prison in America, he found that his release date was scheduled for the same day as Mike Tyson. Marks had spent seven years in prison for attempting to smuggle a benign substance like cannabis into the country. Tyson had served just three years for a brutal rape.[14]

Hypocrisy is rife among anti-drugs campaigners and law enforcers as well. This piece about a police officer in England takes some beating:

> *"Detective Chief Inspector Gerry Dickinson has been fighting drugs since joining the police 28 years ago. The walls of his office are covered with merit awards and commendations, and group photographs with smiling colleagues. There are anti-drug campaign posters too, and a worn-out map of Great Britain. In a prominent place is a certificate: Dickinson is not just the head of the West Yorkshire Police Drug Squad, he is also a qualified Irish whiskey taster. Just like with the whiskey, Dickinson is passionate about his work."* [15]

What can you say to that! Apart from anything else this sort of thing breeds contempt for the police and the law. Can't these people see that? There should be no place for this sort of double standard. To paraphrase the writer William Burroughs: Just Say No To Drugs Hypocrisy.

THE CASE FOR THE DECRIMINALISATION OF DRUG USE

What does decriminalisation of drug use actually mean? And is it the same as legalisation? Going by comments made by opponents of both decriminalisation and legalisation it would seem there is still confusion about their respective meanings. Decriminalisation of drug use means that it would no longer be a criminal or fiscal offence for a person to have in their possession a specified amount of any particular drug for their own personal use. What it *doesn't* mean is legalising the *sale* or *supply* of drugs. That is a separate issue. This needs to be made clear from the start because as soon as anyone suggests a debate on the decriminalisation of drug use politicians and the media invariably try to confuse the issue by presenting it as meaning the legalisation of the sale of drugs.

For example, when the General Assembly for the Church of Scotland called for a Royal Commission to discuss the decriminalisation of cannabis use, the editorial in the next day's *Daily Record* thundered: *"We all know the evils and dangers of drink and smoking. Do we really want another legalised danger in the form of soft drugs?"* [1]

The Scotsman managed to employ four by-lined journalists to come up with an introduction to an article that read: *"Tony Blair last night condemned the Church of Scotland for suggesting the legalisation of cannabis should be considered."* [2]

Whether this was said out of a genuine misunderstanding of the term "decriminalisation," readers can decide for themselves.

IF DRUG USE IS A CRIME THEN WHO IS THE VICTIM OF THAT CRIME?

The case for the decriminalisation of drug use starts with this question. It cuts right to the heart of the drug debate and is an infallible detector of hypocrisy, double-standards and muddled thinking. It's a priority question that needs to be posed to anyone who is still in favour of the current drug laws.

The usual justification for the continued criminality of drug use is given that the victim of the crime is the drug user themselves. Sometimes it is even suggested that all of society is the victim.

But do these reasons stand up to scrutiny?

SOCIETY AS VICTIM

This brings into the drug debate all sorts of questions such as: How far should the state interfere with an individual's personal liberty? What do we do if one person's freedom invades another person's rights? Are we individuals or part of a society? Or to put it another way: Should we be allowed to do whatever the hell we want irrespective of the consequences?

This isn't a new debate. Ancient Greek philosophers such as Plato have wrestled with it, as have modern thinkers such as John Stuart Mill, who in his *Essay On Liberty* questioned others' rights to drink alcohol:

> *"If anything invades my social rights, certainly the traffic in strong drink does. It destroys my primary right of security, by*

constantly creating and stimulating social disorder. It invades my right of equality, by deriving a profit from the creation of a misery I am taxed to support. It impedes my right to free moral and intellectual development, by surrounding my path with dangers, and by weakening and demoralising society, from which I have a right to claim aid and discourse." [3]

This book doesn't have handy ready-made answers to these complex philosophical questions. But it is clear that a balance needs to be found between individual freedoms and the fact that there is such a thing as society.

The taking of drugs does not itself, as an act, create any victims of any crimes. If any acts carried out under the influence of drugs *do* break existing laws then the laws are *already* in place to deal with such offences. The drug is not the offender. It is the person who is responsible. How many times have we heard that drinking alcohol is no excuse for behaviour carried out under its influence. The same goes for illegal drugs.

PERSONAL RISK

Our freedoms are precious. But they aren't written in tablets of stone. Vigilance is necessary to ensure they aren't eroded any further.

One of the freedoms we have in a free society is the freedom to take risks with our own health and our own body so long as it doesn't put anyone else at risk. This isn't a freedom that is written on any statute book but one which already exists in practice. Risk is part and parcel of life.

There is a risk involved when you cross the road – even if the green man is flashing. A lorry or a car may swerve out of control and onto the pavement. What society does through its government, its laws, and its social spending, is it tries to minimise perceived risks by introducing measures like traffic lights, speed limits, drink driving laws, street lighting, etc. These are common-sense, harm reduction measures to reduce the everyday risks of life. Society is always trying to minimise the chances of accidents happening and so it should. The underlying philosophy behind all of this is:

We are primarily social animals, interdependent on each other for many things, and within that context we should collectively do whatever is possible to ensure that everyone should have the choice *of as long and as healthy a life as possible in order to explore life's many possibilities.*

Emphasis however should be on the word *choice*. Freedom is all about choice. Compulsion is the way of dictators.

It could be argued that this is all very well with regards to risks from accidents but why should the rest of society pick up the bill when someone does something that *deliberately* puts themselves at risk. Again, this doesn't stand up beside the facts. Society has *already* decided that people are entitled to take risks with their health, and even with their lives.

There are no serious attempts made to ban such dangerous sports as mountaineering, paragliding, sky diving, motor racing, horse racing, or skiing. Yet all of these put the participant at serious risk of injury or death. A comparison with taking drugs needs to be made if the risk-to-oneself argument is to carry any weight.

Take ecstasy for example. Ecstasy is often cited as a dangerous drug which can kill or damage the user's health. The official number of ecstasy-related deaths in the UK is estimated to be around 7 per year (even allowing for secondary factors, many of which could be avoided, such as from drinking too much water or overheating.) If 500,000 tablets or capsules of ecstasy are taken every week[4] in Britain then the risk of death can easily be calculated:

Comparative Risks of Death:

Taking 1 tablet of ecstasy – 1 death in 3.7 million.[5]
Five rides at a fairground – 1 death in 3.2 million.[6]
A skiing holiday in Switzerland – 1 death in 600,000.[7]
Parachuting – 1 death for every 85,000 jumps. (29 times higher risk than taking an E).[8]
Attempting to climb K2 – 1 in every 4. (Yes, so high it's almost suicide with 37 deaths in 150 attempts.)[9]

Does this mean that we should ban dangerous sports as well? Obviously not. No-one would argue that. The risk of death or serious injury is generally accepted to be part of the activity although attempts are made to minimise these risks wherever possible – without reducing the pleasure that participants get from taking part in them.

Why should taking drugs be any different? In fact, if dangerous sports were analysed closer it could be seen just how similar some of them are to taking drugs.

The pleasure from taking drugs comes from their chemical interaction with various receptors in the brain. Compare this with the rush that comes from driving a racing car at 200mph, or skiing down a slope in the Alps, or leaping out of an aeroplane with a parachute strapped to your back. As with drugs, the buzz actually comes in chemical form, from the body's release of adrenaline. Participants in dangerous sports can quite often become hooked on this buzz – the term "adrenaline junkies" is the one that springs to mind.

Sports injuries cost the public health services a lot of money yet no one grudges paying it. Similarly, mountain rescue teams cost money to operate for what is very much a minority sport. Yet even though it is only a tiny minority of people who attempt to climb imposing mountains in wintry conditions, would we deny these people the right to try? To pit themselves against nature no matter how dangerous it might be? Of course not. Privately we admire their courage.

Clearly, *there is no law against taking dangerous risks*. It is plain hypocrisy and double standards to use risk to the user as a reason for criminalising drug use. More so when you consider that fast cars and dangerous sports tend to be the preserve of the wealthy. Drugs may be the only affordable way of getting that same risky pleasure for a lot of young people living in poverty.

Finally, we have to go back to our old friends alcohol and tobacco. Would anyone in their right mind try to make it a crime to use these drugs because they are dangerous to the users health? Of course not. Just like with dangerous sports the priority is to get over information about the risks involved and to do as much as possible to reduce the harm associated with these activities.

CRIME AND SOCIAL DISORDER

It is also argued that taking drugs is a crime because it leads on to social disorder, violence and other crimes. With the exception of property crimes such as housebreaking and shoplifting (which are dealt with elsewhere) this doesn't bear up to scrutiny. Very few illicit drugs make the user aggressive and anti-social (unless they're mixed with legal drugs like alcohol or tranquillisers.) Ian Hamilton QC commented: *"Most murders are committed by people who have drunk alcohol. Out of the many hundreds I have seen in more than 40 years of advocacy I can't recall one done under the influence of cannabis or ecstasy. These drugs are benign in their effect."* [10]

While most heroin addicts have to steal to fund their habits heroin isn't a drug which makes people aggressive – in fact quite the opposite.

The main drug which is responsible for social disorder and violence is undoubtedly alcohol. In Edinburgh, the area of the city where the club/dance scene is predominantly situated is mainly around the Royal Mile, Cowgate and Old Town. The discos and nightclubs around Lothian Road and the West End of the city tend to be more alcohol-fuelled than centred around ecstasy and dance drugs. The difference is there for anyone to see when the respective clubs empty on a Friday or Saturday night. Just ask a policeman.

In the first few months of 1996 there was one of the periodic "cannabis droughts" which hit Scotland hard. No more so than Glasgow. Hash smokers in the city claimed it was worse than at any other time they could remember. (I'll resist the obvious joke.) Drug agencies and police both reported a significant rise in city centre incidences of violence as some cannabis smokers switched to drugs they normally avoided – such as alcohol mixed with downer drugs like Temazepan (jellies).

Drug taking is a victimless crime. Through the ages there have been other victimless crimes such as homosexuality, prostitution and abortion. And as with these so-called crimes the prosecution of offenders has benefited no-one. These laws have never made any difference to whether people carried on such activities but only succeeded in driving otherwise honest citizens into the hands of the black market or into a disregard for the law and its enforcers.

The only other weapon in the arsenal of those who would oppose decriminalisation of drugs is that it would "send out the wrong message" by saying that it's okay to use them. If this was correct then why is the legality of tobacco not taken as meaning that the government is condoning or promoting cigarette use? Smoking may be legal but it is on the decline as the health education message gets through. There is no contradiction between decriminalising the use of any drug and better drug education about the harm the drug may cause. It is a question of practicality.

There are also some welcome knock-on effects which would come from decriminalising drug use. The climate of fear that surrounds even talking about drug use would be ended. At present, because of the fear of family reactions, fear of losing a job, and fear of discrimination, many drug users won't participate openly in the drug debate which makes the voices of anti-drugs campaigners sound louder and more representative than they really are.

When BBC's Frontline Scotland team made a documentary broadcast in May '96 they couldn't find a single working adult to come forward and put the viewpoint of someone who used drugs but didn't have a problem with them. Yet the survey done in Edinburgh among over 600 drug users found that only 1 per cent stated that they had a problem with their drug use and only 11 per cent used drugs for negative reasons such as escaping from other problems.[11]

To go back to the survey[12] which found that 32 per cent of adults over the age of 18 in Scotland have used illegal drugs, it is completely unacceptable for one third of the Scottish population to be living in fear of what they do privately, unable to come out and talk about it for fear of persecution. What other minority would be treated in such a manner?

CONCLUSION

It may seem contradictory or even self-defeating for a book which goes on to argue for ending the black market in drugs by legalising their *sale* to spend time also arguing for the decriminalisation of drug *use*. Surely the first and preferred option would make the second irrelevant?

Well, there are two separate and pragmatic reasons for this.

Firstly; it is a priority that drug users are not subjected to further persecution for a crime that has no victims. Once the principle of decriminalising all personal drug use has been decided it is a relatively simple matter of specifying how much of any one drug constitutes possession or personal use. With one straightforward act of parliament, victimisation by employers and harassment by the authorities would come to an end, and the veil of fear that surrounds open discussion of drug use would be lifted. Everyone would benefit from a more open society.

Secondly, is the realisation that it is unlikely that any government is going to legalise the sale of drugs without putting its toe in the water first with decriminalisation. Therefore the arguments for decriminalisation have to be made. Just as a devolved parliament in Scotland may at some stage in the future put full independence on the agenda, decriminalisation will almost certainly pave the way for a fuller debate on legalisation.

In Holland, where decriminalisation of cannabis has been practised for over twenty years, there are both advantages and disadvantages with not going the full way to legalisation. The Dutch system is examined in the final chapter of this book.

WHICH DRUGS SHOULD BE TAKEN OUT OF THE BLACK MARKET?

This is the hottest of hot potatoes. This is the one area of politics where even the most intrepid back-bencher usually fears to tread. Whilst decriminalisation of a so-called soft drug like cannabis can gather support from such moderates and pillars of the establishment as The Church of Scotland, The Liberal Democrats, the *Independent on Sunday* newspaper, Ron Clarke (ex-DCI, Greater Manchester Police), Louis Blom-Cooper QC, Jon Snow, Richard Branson and even government ministers (when they haven't been gagged by party leaders), the concept of legalising the production and sale of drugs is seen as one step away from plunging society into chaos and disintegration. Without any rational and informed dissemination of information the idea is dismissed out of hand.

But are these fears justified? Would legalising drugs lead to an increase in their use? Would it mean corner shops selling fifty-seven varieties of drugs including everything from cannabis to heroin? Or is there a sane and rational way to approach the subject?

Instead of advocating the immediate legalisation of every drug and standing back to see what happens, it would make common sense to work out which drugs are causing the biggest problems to society *through their sale and production being controlled by the illegal black market* and use these as the logical starting point.

WHICH DRUGS ARE BEING USED?

Surveys are useful for giving an idea of which drugs are being used and by whom. But the most accurate picture of which illegal drugs are being used comes from the Home Office crime statistics. A breakdown of the most recent statistics on drug seizures and drug offences gives a pretty clear picture of which illegal drugs are being most widely used.

	Number of drug seizures in 1995 (by Customs and Police)[1]		Weight (kg)
Cannabis	91,325	(80%)	58,484
Amphetamines	15,443	(13%)	819
Heroin	6,468	(6%)	1,395
Ecstasy	5,513	(5%)	554,000 (doses)
Cocaine	3,654	(3%)	672
LSD	1,155	(1%)	382,000 (doses)

These figures are surprisingly consistent over the previous ten years with only the proportional use of ecstasy on the increase (slightly) and cannabis on the decrease (slightly – from 82% in 1985). (NB Some drug seizures were of more than one drug hence the total seizures is over 100%).

	Number of Persons found guilty, cautioned or dealt with by compounding (fined)[2]	
Cannabis	76,694	(82%)
Amphetamines	10,364	(11%)
Heroin	4,219	(5%)
Ecstasy	3,821	(4%)
Cocaine	2,073	(2%)
LSD	1,268	(1%)

There are some important conclusions which can be drawn from comparing these two sets of data.

1) Cannabis is the illicit drug that dominates the market. It is the illicit drug which is used most and is imported in the biggest quantities. It is also the drug which is criminalising the most people.

2) Britain is not awash with hundreds of different drugs. Only six illicit drugs are being sold in any quantity on the black market. These are the six illicit drugs which are currently enriching the crime syndicates. It follows (for the reasons given in Chapter 2) that these are the six drugs which initially need to be removed from the black market. (To these should also be included hallucinogenic magic mushrooms since their popularity is not reflected in the quantity of seizures or convictions for use or sale as most people pick their own – although it *is* a criminal offence to prepare them for use or to sell them on.)

3) Should the removal of any of these drugs from the black market see the rise in the black market trade of any other illicit drugs then the case would also have to be made for taking those drugs out of the black market. Once the *principal* of removing all drugs from the black market has been established first, then the practicalities and the order in which this is to be done can be evaluated.

THE BIG TWO – HEROIN AND CANNABIS

The two drugs causing the most concern, in different ways, and which should immediately be removed from the black market are cannabis and heroin. It is these two drugs which are enriching the criminal underworld more than any others. As can be seen from the above figures it is cannabis which accounts for 80 per cent of drug seizures and over 80 per cent of drug offences. If the sale of cannabis was licensed then the criminalisation associated with illegal drugs in the UK would immediately fall by four-fifths.

Heroin on the other hand, has a much smaller number of users, implicated in only 5 per cent of drug offences. Yet the addictive nature of the drug, its inflated price on the black market, and the fact that it accounts for over 90 per cent of notified drug addictions[3] mean that it needs to be treated as a special case – or even a priority case. The most effective way by which heroin could be successfully removed from the black market could be quite different from that with cannabis.

How this can be done practically – following on from successful experiments elsewhere – as well as practical proposals for removing other drugs from the black market, are dealt with in the remainder of this book.

HEROIN – A SPECIAL CASE,
A PRIORITY CASE

Heroin is the enigma. Of all the illicit drugs in common usage it is heroin that causes the most widespread concern. It isn't surprising, given the number of scare stories and myths surrounding the drug, that for the majority of people who have had little or no contact with heroin's clandestine sub-culture it is a substance shrouded in mystery: its allure is unfathomable; its users are perceived as hopeless junkies; and its consequences seem to be an insoluble downward spiral of addiction, deceit, crime, degradation, despair and in many cases, death.

But for heroin users it is the ultimate drug. It has been said that heroin has a seductive, all-embracing appeal which little else – chemical or otherwise – can emulate. Its initial euphoric high is followed by an inner warmth, a sensuality, and sense of well-being which supposedly surpasses anything that everyday reality has to offer. Unfortunately, as for every other drug, there's always some sort of payback. In the case of heroin the payback is in direct proportion to the pleasures of the drug. Not only do the pleasurable effects of the drug diminish as the body becomes more tolerant to it, heroin can eventually become so physically and mentally addictive that prolonged use becomes an all-consuming battle just to hold at arm's length the effects of withdrawal. The drug takes over.

Heroin needs to be understood. While much of the hysteria

surrounding heroin use badly needs to be put into perspective, trying to get to grips with the drug is absolutely vital; one of the most important issues in the whole drug debate. Understanding the appeal of heroin and, crucially, embracing a practical strategy that effectively removes it from the black market, holds the key to unlocking most of the pressing health and social problems associated with drug use in this country.

HEROIN CHIC?

When the film *Trainspotting* hit the cinema screens in February '96, despite the intentions of all concerned with its production, the anti-hero Renton played by Ewan McGregor – a good-looking, glamorous actor and hardly the archetypal junkie – became a national icon. In the wake of the movie, style magazines like *The Face*, *iD*, and *Blah Blah Blah* ran fashion shoots featuring gaunt skinny models in deliberately scruffy clothing which were obviously based on the idea of so-called "heroin chic." It was said that people who should have known better were inadvertently creating positive images of the drug that could only add to its mystique and allure. And it didn't take long for fingers to point at the movie for being responsible for an increase in the popularity of heroin. Even Presidential candidate Bob Dole jumped on the bandwagon and slammed *Trainspotting* in the 1996 US election campaign.

But is it really credible that the *Trainspotting* factor could be responsible for an increase in the use of heroin as has been suggested? Are young people so gullible they'd start taking smack just because Renton looks cool on their bedroom walls? It hardly seems likely . . . in and of itself. Needless to say, the timing of the movie's release coincided with other more powerful factors which were at work.

HEROIN – A MODERN PLAGUE?

The fact is, heroin has never gone away, nor is it some new phenomenon. The use of opiates goes back thousands of years. When Homer wrote his epic poem *The Odyssey* (700 BC) he referred to a mysterious drug called *nepenthes* "which lulled all pain and gave forgetfulness of grief. No one that swallowed this dissolved in wine could shed a single tear that day, even for the death of his mother and father."[1]

Whilst there has been much debate among historians over the precise identity of *nepenthes*, there was only one drug around at the time *The Odyssey* was written which could have produced such an effect – and that was opium.

Whilst there are numerous examples from history which suggest that opium was taken for many centuries before Homer wrote his famous epic, it was the Greek doctor Hippocrates, the father of modern medicine, who first stated categorically, in the fifth century BC, that the juice from the opium poppy was useful as a narcotic painkiller.

Aristotle's pupil, Theophrastus, is accredited with the first detailed account of how to slit an opium poppy to obtain the drug: "The poppy is the only plant from which the juice is extracted from the head; this is peculiar to it."[2]

Opium was used as a narcotic for another two thousand years before Thomas De Quincy wrote in 1821 what was to become the first modern classic of drug literature, *Confessions of an English Opium-Eater*: "O heavens! what a revulsion! what a resurrection," was how he described his initial joy upon discovering the pleasures of opium, "what an apocalypse of the world within me!" De Quincy would later write of the pain and "shadowy terrors" of addiction.

But it was the scientific advances of the nineteenth century rather than literature which became the catalyst for further widespread use of this powerful, euphoria-producing sedative. In 1898, chemists searching for a more powerful and more effective pain killer than cocaine synthesised heroin from the juice of opium poppies. And with the scientists who discovered nuclear fission, once the genie was out of the bottle, there was no way in which to put it back in.

Heroin continues to be used to this day as the most effective and useful painkiller known to man, giving relief to thousands of cancer sufferers as well as countless other medical patients – including women in childbirth who are injected with a pure pharmaceutical form of heroin called dio-morphine. This alone gives lie to the idea that heroin is an "evil" substance. However, it is when it has been abused as a recreational drug that heroin gives rise to concern.

SMACK IS BACK?

After the sustained media blitz against ecstasy following the death of Leah Betts, it was inevitable that the press would assume their readership had wearied of the subject. They'd have to find something else to scare the living daylights out of the public. Devil dogs, food bugs, mad cow disease, religious sects, rabies, schizophrenics, global warming, comets hitting Earth, joyriders – all of these have had their fifteen minutes worth of exaggeration and hype. It was time to return with a new angle to the British media's favourite scare story: the drug menace. And what better way to follow on the back of the hit movie *Trainspotting* than digging up some anecdotal evidence in order to proclaim that "smack is back".

But for once, despite the exaggerations and complete lack of understanding as to why this was happening, the tabloid press were actually right. There had been a significant rise in the use of heroin. There were any number of reputable sources who could testify to this.

In 1991 there were 4,883 heroin addicts notified to the Home Office. By 1994 this had more than doubled to 10,067.[3] This was broadly in line with the trend of heroin seizures. In 1991 police and customs seized 490 kilos of heroin. In 1995 this had almost trebled to 1,390 kilos.[4] Clearly there was a supply-led influx of cheap heroin taking place instigated not by any movies that might be showing on British screens but by the international crime syndicates importing it in ever greater quantities.

The effects of the flood of cheap heroin soon became noticeable on the streets. A report at the end of 1995 from a West Yorkshire drug agency, Unit 51, stated ominously: *"We've got something serious on our hands and we need to do something about it now. If we don't, it will become an epidemic."* [5]

Unit 51 had seen 1000 clients in 1995 and around 100 of them had been heroin users in their teens or under. Unit 51's Colin Wisely commented:

"It used to send a panic around a drug agency if we saw someone so young on heroin, but it's reached the stage now where it's become normal ... Heroin has become fashionable and acceptable amongst the young. A few years ago new drug users were more discerning and wouldn't have touched heroin – it was seen as a loser's drug." [6]

All across the country similar stories came in of alarm and concern. An article in Community Care highlighted the problem of a significant increase in heroin use in rural areas.[7] A drug worker in one such rural area in the south of England told Druglink:

"Smack is just swimming around this village, it's phenomenal.

Most of the young people here use heroin on a recreational basis."

A similar picture emerged in Scotland. In Glasgow's Possil estate, during the cannabis drought of early 1996, heroin wraps were available for ten pounds each or three for twenty quid. "Dial-a-Wrap" services complete with business cards and mobile phone numbers appeared in some areas of the country as dealers got more aggressive and competitive in their marketing of the drug. There was particular concern about heroin use in some rural areas of Scotland – most noticeably in the north-east around Aberdeen. Grampian police estimated a dramatic ten-fold increase in the use of heroin in a single year. In Edinburgh, the drug agency Crew 2000 felt concerned enough to produce their first harm reduction advice leaflet on heroin aimed primarily at young clubbers.

Clearly, heroin use is on the increase. But, like every other drug-related issue, a sense of perspective and a clear understanding of where the problem lies is important. Blind panic usually ends up with a draconian crackdown by the authorities which hasn't been thought through properly, and almost always ends up exacerbating the problem.

SO WHAT EXACTLY IS THE EXTENT OF THE HEROIN PROBLEM?

The Addict Index published in *Druglink* is one of the most useful indicators of where the drug problem lies in the UK. It charts the notification of addicts. While the actual numbers of addicts are far from exact, since it is estimated that only around 10 to 20 per cent of addicts notify the medical authorities, the overall trends can still be established.

In 1979, 65 per cent of all those drug addicts notified were addicted to heroin and 70 per cent of new addicts notified were for heroin.[8] This was before the floodgates opened up in the early years of the Thatcher Government. By 1986, the figures had risen to 90 and 91 per cent respectively. By 1994, heroin users made up 87 per cent of all notified addicts and 93 per cent of all new addicts notified.[9] (These figures exclude addiction to prescribed drugs like methadone.) It also follows that if nine out of ten addicts in this country – addicted to illicit drugs – are addicted to heroin, then the conclusion must be that we have a heroin problem in the UK rather than a general drug problem.

Comparing all of these reports and figures, it would seem that the "smack is back" type headlines are somewhat wide of the mark. Smack has never really gone away. It is the scale of the problem that has increased. The number of notified heroin addicts has trebled to 22,000 in the eight years up to 1994.[10] The actual figure for the number of heroin addicts in UK has been estimated as high as 20,000 by some drug agencies.[11] And rising. Alarm bells certainly should be ringing at the failure of existing methods in dealing with this.

HEROIN ADDICTION AND CRIME

The city of Glasgow, with its sprawling urban housing estates and high levels of unemployment, accounts for 8,500 of Scotland's estimated 20,000 intravenous heroin addicts.[12] Alarmingly this is one per cent of the city's entire population. Glasgow has the unwanted honour of having the youngest average age of heroin injectors in the world at just sixteen years old.[13] There are heroin injectors in places like Castlemilk and Possil as young as ten.

In 1995, 102 people died in Glasgow as a result of injecting heroin, methadone or a heroin cocktail.[14] Anyway you want to look at it, Glasgow has a serious problem with heroin use.

A report drawn up by health and drug workers gave a stark

account of the economic cost of sustaining such a high level of heroin addiction: it calculated that £500 million worth of crimes need to be committed every year to feed Glasgow's 8,500 heroin habits.[15]

The report reckoned that these 8,500 addicts spend an average of £300 per week on heroin and prescription drugs, which comes to a total of £130 million per year.[16] Strathclyde Police have calculated that of the annual drug bill of £130 million, around three-quarters, or £100 million, comes from vehicle and property crime. And since goods sold on the black market only fetch around 20 per cent of their retail value, addicts end up having to steal £500 million of goods every year to feed their addictions.

At the time, Detective Inspector Eddie McColm, Strathclyde Police's Deputy Drugs Co-ordinator, said: *"The figure of £500 million doesn't surprise me, but it will raise quite a few eyebrows."*[17]

A Home Office report of May '97 claimed that one in five crimes are committed by people on heroin.[18] They estimated that around £1.3 billion of goods are stolen each year to pay for heroin addiction. This would seem to be vastly underestimating the true figure if the Glasgow report is even half accurate. The overall UK cost to Joe Public and local businesses in terms of property crime is more likely to be around £8-10 billion per annum.[19]

It has been increasingly recognised that addicts can't be left to live a life of crime to pay for their habits. It is tearing apart the fabric of society in many areas.

METHADONE IN THEIR MADNESS?

For a large part of the 1980s Edinburgh had a serious problem with heroin. Shared needles and a shooting gallery sub-culture had contributed to an unprecedented spread of HIV infection, so much so that the city's bedsit-land and peripheral housing estates became home to a spiralling epidemic. Concern was quickly transforming itself into panic and something had to be done. Fast.

Despite a public outcry at the time Edinburgh introduced a number of measures to try and halt the spread of the virus. The first of these was a system of clean needle exchanges which injecting heroin users could use to discard old works and pick up new ones. Critics at the time claimed this pioneering harm reduction policy was encouraging drug use. Given the tragic consequences of that first wave of HIV infection, those critics of needle exchanges now sound both reactionary and foolish, akin to Nero fiddling while Rome burnt.

In 1988, to try and stem the spread of HIV infection – as well as the rising number of heroin-related deaths from overdose through adulterated and badly-cut street drugs – the authorities in Edinburgh, led by Lothian Health Board, began prescribing methadone to heroin addicts. (Methadone is a synthetic heroin substitute which is usually prescribed as a green liquid and is taken orally to keep at bay the unpleasant withdrawal symptoms.) It was hoped that this policy would reduce the rate of HIV infection, reduce the number of addicts injecting, reduce drug-related crime, and in doing so would stabilise the lives of addicts as they tried to get to grips with their addiction.

The results seemed to bear this out. Roger Lewis, director of the Edinburgh centre which monitors HIV, AIDS, and drug addiction stated: *"Running with the harm-reduction model has worked. Last year in Edinburgh only 10 per cent of addicts were injecting."* [20]

Lothian and Borders Police Force also attributed a 30 per cent fall in property-related crimes in the area to the methadone maintenance programme.[21] Edinburgh's methadone programme has been praised by the Government and the all-party Commons Select Committee on Scottish Affairs as the best way of keeping addicts alive and cutting drug-related crime.

The authorities in Glasgow, where heroin has again taken a grip, were criminally slow off the mark. It wasn't until 1994 that Greater Glasgow Health Board introduced the methadone programme and those wasted years of procrastination proved disastrous. Myopic politicians and vociferous anti-drugs campaigners combined forces to allow the city's heroin problem to spread rapidly. As stated previously, by 1996 the city had become the world's heroin capital with the youngest average age of injecting drug users anywhere in the world.

However, the introduction of the harm reduction programmes quickly proved their usefulness. The wisdom of needle sharing is now rarely questioned and the rate of spread of HIV infection has slowed down.

By the start of 1996 1,700 addicts in Glasgow had opted onto the methadone programme.[22] GGHB's Dr Laurence Gruer, a co-author of the report into drug-related crime said: *"There's plenty of evidence that those 1,700 people are committing fewer crimes. Some claim to have stopped criminal activity altogether ... So I would expect the figures of £130 million and £500 million to go down."* [23]

Detective Inspector McColm concurred: *"My perception is that crimes associated with drug abusers – shoplifting, street robbery, housebreaking and car crime – have gone down in the last year."* [24]

More recent estimations suggest Glasgow's 8,500 injecting drug users may have fallen by as much as a half with up to 2,500 addicts now on the methadone scheme.[25]

Although the methadone programme can claim to have been relatively useful for many addicts the project still has critics pointing out its deficiencies. There are those who believe the methadone programme is counter-productive. They point to studies in America presented to America's House of Representatives Select Committee on Narcotics Abuse and Control that up to 50 per cent of methadone patients at some publicly funded drug clinics were continuing to use other illicit drugs such as heroin and cocaine.[26]

Such allegations would seem to bear up under scrutiny in Scotland where the resale of prescribed methadone is well-documented. If the authorities had bothered to ask the heroin addicts themselves what they thought should be done, they might have got some interesting and important answers.

Heroin addicts interviewed by the *Sunday Times* made it clear what they thought of methadone.[27]

One addict commented: *"For six months I took it, going to the chemist to collect it but all it did was give me a kick-start in the morning before I went and got other stuff."*

Another said she needed stimulants to counteract the lethargic feeling she got from her methadone prescription, adding: *"Two mates of mine have come off (methadone), and one went back to heroin straight off. I don't know what to do but I don't want methadone."*

In the course of researching this book I spoke to a number of heroin addicts and ex-addicts groups who were virtually unanimous that although they were prepared to use the methadone treatment programme, it wasn't methadone that they needed. They said that methadone made them lethargic, that it didn't give them any buzz, and that, crucially, it was more addictive than heroin and therefore harder to get off.

Many addicts are selling on their methadone to get money for heroin. One extremely dubious attempt at getting round this problem has been adopted in the Greater Glasgow area. A system of supervision has been put in operation since 1994 where 60 per cent of the community pharmacists in the city have agreed to observe the patient swallowing their daily dose on their premises, usually six days a week.[28] This "solution" has been pushed to every general practitioner in the area, with GGHB urging them to bring it into operation for at least the first year of treatment. In other words force-feed the addicts with a drug they don't want.

Apart from the dubious ethics of this policy addicts can be resourceful when it comes to deception. They have to be just to get the money for their habits. There have been reports of a trade in what has been called "spit methadone" where addicts puke up their methadone into a bag once they leave the pharmacy or clinic and then sell it on.[29]

Others simply use methadone to keep withdrawal symptoms at bay while they search for heroin or money to buy heroin.

There are other serious problems with methadone. Methadone is a highly toxic substance. Much more so than even adulterated street heroin. In the ten years from 1982-1991, for example, there were 243 recorded heroin deaths and 349 recorded methadone deaths.[30] In 1991, there were 77 methadone deaths notified and 44 heroin deaths.[31]

A comparison of methadone and heroin deaths shows an even more alarming cause for concern. In 1991, it was estimated that there was a total addict population in the UK of 123,500 of which 113,620 were heroin addicts and around 9,880 methadone addicts.[32] Calculations suggest that the mortality rate for heroin addicts in 1991 was 1 in 2,582; while the mortality rate for methadone addicts was 1 in 134. Thus methadone would appear to be 19 times more toxic than even adulterated street heroin which is cut with all sorts of substances and is sold in unidentifiable strengths.

A team of doctors carrying out a Scottish Office analysis of drug deaths in Edinburgh and Glasgow have found similar evidence of the dangers of methadone. In 1996 45 people all under the age of 30 died in Edinburgh after taking methadone. In the first three months of 1997 another 20 young people have died from taking methadone in the Scottish capital.[33] That is 20 out of an overall total of 30 drug deaths in the area.

The problem seems to be that many of Edinburgh's 1,500 registered addicts who are prescribed methadone are selling it on to buy heroin, according to Lothian and Borders Police. The purchasers are young drug-takers whose bodies are unable to cope with such a toxic substance. Some deaths have been people using methadone for the first time or ex-prisoners released from jail who have lost their former tolerance to the drug and have died taking their first fix after being released.

The case against methadone is strong. Metropolitan Police surgeons have stated that methadone it is sold to fund purchases of heroin. Even its manufacturers say it is not recommended as being suitable for "detoxing" patients because it is too addictive.[34] It is proven to be highly dangerous. And addicts don't want it. So why persist in prescribing it? Why not just prescribe what heroin addicts need most until they're ready to come off – which is heroin.

HEROIN ON PRESCRIPTION

The idea of handing out free heroin to addicts sticks in the throats of many anti-drugs campaigners. David Bryce, founder of Calton Athletic drug rehabilitation support group is one prominent critic of the idea.

> *"The idea comes from academics and policy-makers with absolutely no personal experience. They go to seminars where phoneys tell them 'we have to give addicts what they want to help.' All addicts want are more drugs. It's tragic and defeatist; there's been an increase in resources but it is not working. They have created an atmosphere where streetwise kids can work the system."*[35]

Bryce believes that addicts should just stop using drugs. And that there should be facilities like Calton Athletic to help them do that. But the logic of this is that *until* addicts are ready to give up drugs they should be left at the mercy of the criminal underworld who control the supply of the drugs, and they should risk death with heroin of unknown strength or composition while living a life of crime and squalor in order to pay for these drugs. What is tragic and defeatist is refusing to recognise that addiction is a medical problem that needs medical treatment.

While Calton Athletic deserves funding and recognition for the work it does, this approach based on cold turkey withdrawal just doesn't work for everyone. It isn't just a question of resources, either, although these are woefully inadequate in Scotland. The problem is that heroin addicts need to be mentally ready to come off the drug. If they were ready to go cold turkey then addicts would be battering at the doors of groups like Calton Athletic in their thousands every day. Most aren't.

What Bryce and other prominent anti-drugs campaigners refuse to recognise is that there needs to be a range of options available to help addicts either come off heroin directly or to stabilise their lives until they are ready to come off. Addicts are individuals and what suits one person's personality needn't necessarily suit the next person. This has to be taken into account.

And just as importantly, it isn't only the addicts themselves that need to be considered but the local communities they live in. Residents of towns, villages and cities where heroin use has become a problem need a break from the crime, housebreaking, drug wars and street dealers. If heroin was taken off the streets and put in supervised clinics everyone in the area would benefit.

This is the thinking behind the idea of prescribing pure pharmaceutical heroin to registered addicts instead of methadone. But would it work in practice?

THE WIDNES EXPERIMENT

Over the last 12 years, a bold, pioneering experiment has taken place around Widnes, Merseyside. Pure pharmaceutical heroin was prescribed to registered addicts under the guidance of clinical psychiatrist Dr John Marks.

The results of this experiment may well hold the key to effectively tackling a problem that has left politicians, police and health workers completely impotent in the face of a renewed surge in heroin use across the country. A fanciful claim? Consider the facts.

In 1985, as part of a strategy to stop the spread of HIV infection on Merseyside, a number of harm reduction policies were initiated. Needle exchanges was one. But probably the most innovative was the policy of prescribing a drug maintenance programme to addicts in Widnes. This extended beyond prescribing just heroin. Cocaine was prescribed to cocaine addicts, amphetamines to amphetamine addicts, etc. The system was flexible enough to cater for the needs of individuals but rigid enough to carefully monitor the results.

Until 1992, fewer than 1.5 per cent of notified drug addicts on Merseyside had contracted HIV.[36] This was proportionally the lowest rate of infection in the UK despite Merseyside having the highest rate of addiction in the country. This was impressive but it was the results of the unique work in Widnes that was making people really sit up and take notice:[37]

- Up to the pivotal year of 1990 when the Widnes experiment was forced to backtrack, police reported a 15-fold (96 per cent) reduction in acquisitive crime. Addicts no longer needed to rob to pay for their fix.

- Locally acquired HIV infection from drug use was zero. This despite Liverpool having an above average proportion of drug users.
- With heroin now available in the clinic, the gangsters who oversaw the black market no longer had a clientele and there was a reported 12-fold (92 per cent) reduction in new cases of addiction.
- Heroin deaths were zero. Overdosing on suspect street drugs was eradicated.

Dr Marks and the Widnes Drug Dependency Clinic were successful in getting heroin off the streets and stabilising the lives of addicts after all the efforts of law enforcers, anti-drug campaigners and health professionals before them had failed.

An indication of the experiment's success came when the local Marks and Spencer's store was so impressed by the drop in shoplifting that the manager donated £2,000 in 1991 to help finance the UK's first harm reduction conference.[38]

The police were happy, the local community whose cars and houses weren't being broken into were happy, local businesses were happy, and the addicts were getting on with their lives. Merseyside's Regional Health Authorities were justifiably proud of their success and promised lavishing funding to continue with it. In fact, the only ones unhappy were the local drug dealers who no longer had a market for their product.

SO WHY WASN'T THIS ADOPTED AS THE WAY FORWARD ACROSS THE WHOLE COUNTRY?

Standing foursquare with the drug-dealing Liverpool gangsters were voices in the British government who weren't so happy about this perceived policy of "free drugs for junkies." A documentary produced by "World In Action" in April 1990 juxtaposed images of Dr Marks signing a prescription for cocaine with Margaret Thatcher forcibly condemning drug legalisation at a United Nations Conference in London. There was also a diplomatic storm when national TV in the United States broadcast a favourable news report on the Widnes experiment just as George Bush was whipping up support for a global military offensive against drugs. International pressure was put on the UK government behind the scenes. The politicians viewed the Widnes clinic's work as surplus to requirement in the overall war on drugs.

The in-favour policy of methadone maintenance was imposed on the Hope Street clinic which also prescribed heroin in 1989 and, after a delay where methadone was opposed by Dr Marks and most of the addicts themselves, Widnes finally succumbed to it in 1995. The official reason given was cost.

Since then there has been a wall of silence erected around the success of putting heroin on prescription. Harm reduction has subsequently become a diluted and almost meaningless term banded about by anyone who supports needle exchanges or methadone programmes. As could have been predicted the dealers have now moved back into the local areas around Widnes, HIV infection has increased, and there has been a number of heroin and methadone related deaths in the area.

But all is not lost. A controlled heroin prescribing experiment was introduced in Switzerland in 1994, based on the Widnes experience. Official eyes have been watching its progress with interest. With a population of just seven million, Switzerland has long had some of the highest rates of heroin addiction in Europe. Now, out of an estimated 30,000 heroin addicts in Switzerland, 1,000 addicts have been put on a scheme where they receive prescribed heroin from the state.[39] These addicts have been reported as now having stable homes and jobs with a marked improvement in their health while drug-related crime has dropped. Dr Robert Haemig, who is charge of heroin prescription in Berne, believes his first priority is to stop heroin deaths: *"If I can prevent people from dying on the streets by prescribing heroin to them then I am ethically bound to do so."*[40]

Eveline, a 39 year old patient of Dr Haemig, explained why it had worked for her: *"I get up at seven, I have a shower, and I make coffee. Then I stop by the hospital for my injection before going on to work."* Three years previously she had been homeless, begging and stealing, and weighed only six stones. Now she has a flat and a steady job in a restaurant. Three years on the scheme has seen her daily heroin intake reduced from 600mg to 200mg. After ten years of heroin addiction, and thanks to the heroin prescription scheme, she says she is ready to have her maintenance dose reduced to 10mg and then onto being clean.[41]

Despite attacks from the usual suspects, the official Swiss health ministry defended their scheme: *"Where do you want habitual addicts to get their heroin? From the Mafia, or in a controlled scheme, supervised by doctors."* Most importantly of all, *unlike in the UK*, the Swiss government has reported that levels of heroin addiction are now finally dropping.[42] Final confirmation of the popularity of the scheme came in the first week of October 1997 when a national referendum in Switzerland gave the scheme overwhelming backing.

It is worth stating that in Switzerland, like Holland, heroin addicts are left in peace by the police and their habits are sustained by doctors. They are viewed with sympathy and toleration just like any other sick people. Suffice to say, there is little glamour attached to heroin use there, and users certainly aren't viewed as outsiders or rebels. This has been cited as a factor in why heroin use is falling among young people in both these countries.

The time has come to reconsider the British approach to heroin and learn the lessons of the past.

From 1920 to 1967, prescribing heroin to addicts was generally known as "the British system". When the Dangerous Drugs Bill was passed in 1966 effectively putting an end to the British method, a letter printed in *The Times* on November 15th of that year by reader A.J. Hawes predicted that ending the practice of prescribing heroin to addicts would only tempt and encourage the importers of heroin on a large scale.

On June 22nd, 1967, the same A.J. Hawes wrote back to *The Times*:

> *"During the past few weeks I hear from my heroin addict friends that the drug is now appearing on the black market in powder form, which has never been available before. Tablets have always been the form of the drug in this country. It looks as if my dismal prophecy of large-scale heroin merchants waiting their opportunity of a shortage in the black market which has been fed up to now by wicked over-prescribing "junkie" doctors has come to fulfilment."* [43]

His predictions were uncannily shrewd. Two brutal sets of statistics say it all:

In 1967 there were only 1,299 officially notified heroin addicts the UK. By 1994 this had risen to 22,000. [44]

In 1973, customs and police seized 3.2 kilos of heroin. By 1995 this had risen to 1,390 kilos. [45]

In short, Mr A.J. Hawes and all those medical practitioners who predicted such a disaster have been proven absolutely correct. Those in power at that time who oversaw the end to heroin prescription – politicians such as Harold Wilson and James Callaghan

HEROIN SEIZURES BY CUSTOMS AND POLICE

Year	Number	Weight (kg)
1973	N/A	3.2
1974	N/A	2.7
1975	N/A	6.9
1976	350	20.2
1977	N/A	26.5
1978	350	60.8
1979	600	45
1980	700	38
1981	800	93
1982	1000	200
1983	1900	250
1984	3000	360
1985	3200	365
1986	2750	220
1987	2050	240
1988	2200	240
1989	2700	350
1990	2600	600
1991	2600	490
1992	3000	550
1993	3700	650
1994	4500	750
1995	6330	1,390

Source: Home Office Statistical Bulletins
Statistics of Drug Seizures and Offenders Dealt With, United Kingdom, 1973–1995

– should shoulder the full responsibility of the heroin epidemic that has been allowed to happen – and all its attendant horrors.

The case for putting heroin back onto prescription for addicts is unanswerable.

WHAT ABOUT THE FUTURE?

Heroin is a painkiller first and foremost. And an exceptionally useful one at that. But in many ways, the so-called recreational use of heroin should also be considered as a social painkiller. Heroin is frequently used to blot out the pain of unemployment, lack of a future, stress, relationship break-ups and boredom. These are emotional forms of pain. Putting heroin on prescription would undoubtedly stabilise the situation and buy time to tackle the immediate problems of existing addicts.

The root cause of much of the demand for heroin and other painkilling "blocking" drugs such as tranquillisers and sedatives can be traced back to the psychological impact of poverty, bad social conditions, and lack of a decent future. How else do you explain that 94 per cent of heroin addicts in Glasgow are unemployed?[46]

In some areas, particularly in rural communities outwith the central belt of Scotland, it is true that boredom, even among those in work, has been a factor in the rise of heroin use. Facilities for young people are needed as much as jobs and decent houses. Local authority cutbacks are only exacerbating the situation. It is tackling these fundamental social issues that will marginalise the attraction that heroin and other "blocking" drugs have at present. These are the real long-term answers to the heroin problem, and the ones that present the biggest challenge to politicians and public alike.

LICENSING THE SALE
OF CANNABIS

Cannabis hemp is an amazing plant. Apart from its use as a recreational drug, cannabis hemp plants are a natural and ecological source of all sorts of materials from engine oil and soap, to clothing, rope and paper. Even food. For example, at New York's Galaxy restaurant, diners can sample hemp waffles, a tomato sauce made with hemp-seed oil, or even apple pie with a hemp crust. London diners too can tuck into hemp cakes at Café Pushkar or pop into Selfridges for a can of Hemp juice. Apparently, these are healthy foods because of their richness in essential fatty acids.

Cannabis hemp is getting trendy too. Woody Harrelson turned up at the 1997 Oscar ceremonies wearing a hemp tuxedo designed by Giorgio Armani. The British House of Hemp is showing that gone are the days of scratchy hemp shirts. Even Adidas are producing hemp trainers.

The usefulness of hemp has never been in doubt. Canvas sails, hemp ropes, hemp paper, and hemp fuel have been used for centuries. Even the most ardent of anti-cannabis presidents, George Bush, owes his life to cannabis hemp technology. When he was shot down in the Second World War in the Far East it was a parachute made of hemp that floated him down to safety. And hemp ropes that pulled him out of the sea.

The uses of cannabis hemp throughout history could fill a book (and have). The original draft of the American Declaration of Independence was signed on hemp paper. As was the first printing done of the Gutenberg Bible. There was even a time in America (1763-67) when hemp was in such short supply that you could be jailed in the state of Virginia for NOT growing cannabis plants.

In 1942 when the Japanese invaded the Philippines – who supplied America with most of its hemp – the American government sent 400,000 pounds of cannabis hemp seeds to American farmers along with war posters proclaiming "Hemp For Victory!" Subsequently, 42,000 tonnes of hemp fibre were produced annually in the United States until 1946.[1]

(It should be pointed out that all of the above products can be produced from cannabis hemp plants which have little or no active psychoactive ingredients like THC – the substance which is mainly responsible for the high when it is smoked or ingested.)

Cannabis can also be used as a versatile medicine. It has been proven to help sufferers of such diverse illnesses as glaucoma, ME, MS, anorexia, epilepsy, period pains, and as an appetite stimulant for individuals suffering from such illnesses as AIDS. The British Medical Association backed the call for recognition of the medical use of cannabis at their 1997 conference in Edinburgh.[2]

You would be hard pushed to find another plant grown anywhere in the world whose usefulness gets even near to that of cannabis. Yet in the US, cannabis cultivation is still banned. In the UK, cannabis production has only recently been licensed for the growing of THC-free hemp. The medical and recreational uses of cannabis are still outlawed.

The ongoing campaign to recognise the medical uses of cannabis is an important one which, if successful, will not only bring relief to thousands of sufferers but would also mean an end to the criminalisation of those who have to go to the black market to procure it for them. That such a situation still arises is completely outrageous.

However, it is with regards to the legalisation of the sale of cannabis as a recreational drug that this section is primarily concerned.

CANNABIS USE

Cannabis was a bit of a late-comer to British shores. Although it was banned in the UK in 1939 – two years after the United States – until the beginning of the 1950s its use hadn't really spread. Its rise in popularity was largely intertwined with the wave of Afro-Caribbean migrant labour that Britain had encouraged and welcomed here after the war as well as a growing youth culture which was enthusiastically embracing the black music of jazz, blues and rock'n'roll.

Smoking of cannabis rapidly became popular among white youth in the UK. So much so, that by 1964 more whites than blacks were being convicted of cannabis offences and cannabis had become part of an alternative underground culture.[3]

Today cannabis use cuts across race and class boundaries. Cannabis smoking has become one of Britain's favourite recreational pastimes. In the UK there are an estimated 6-7 million cannabis smokers.[4] Among teenagers the numbers are even higher. A UK-wide survey estimated that one in three 14 & 15 year olds have tried cannabis and that 70 per cent of this age group knew of at least one cannabis dealer.[5] In Scotland, it was estimated that over half (53 per cent) of all school leavers have tried cannabis.[6]

It stands to reason that in any given society you cannot have such a huge number of individuals taking part in such a clandestine and illegal activity without the legal foundations of that society being seriously undermined. This is exactly what cannabis prohibition is doing.

There has also been a sea change in attitudes towards cannabis. The *13th British Social Attitudes* report found that public disapproval of cannabis smoking was declining rapidly. 82 per cent of British people thought smoking cannabis should remain illegal in 1983. Ten years later this had dropped to 58 per cent.[7]

As this book was about to go to print a poll published in the *Independent on Sunday* (12 October '97) found that 80 per cent of those surveyed wanted the law on cannabis to be relaxed with only 17 per cent in favour of the status quo. A poll in the *Daily Mirror* the same week (11 October '97) found that nearly two-thirds of those surveyed were in favour of decriminalisation of cannabis. This refutes the idea that the current drug laws on cannabis have majority support.

A HEAVY PRICE TO PAY

In 1967 a famous advert appeared in *The Times* newspaper[8] which stated that "the law against marijuana is immoral in principle and unworkable in practice." It was signed by such prominent figures of the time as The Beatles, Brian Walden MP, David Dimbleby, David Hockney and Graham Greene. It caused a big enough impact for the government to set up a Home Office select committee to examine the arguments.

Chaired by Baroness Wootton, the government's select committee made some sensible recommendations – based on scientific and reliable evidence – that cannabis was no more harmful than tobacco or alcohol, and that it was a mistake to regard cannabis as similar to heroin and cocaine. The committee recommended that possession should no longer be viewed as a serious crime.

Unfortunately, the government of the day rejected these findings and cannabis users have been criminalised ever since.

Since the advert appeared in 1967 – up to the end of 1995 – 651,308 persons have been found guilty, cautioned or dealt with by pounding (fined) for cannabis offences. This is 84.2% of a total of 773,581 drug offenders dealt with in the last 28 years.[9]

	All drug offences	Cannabis offences	Percentage (cannabis)[10]
1969–1995	773,581	651,308	84.2%
1969	6,911	4,683	68%
1975	11,603	8,987	77%
1985	26,958	21,737	81%
1995	93,631	76,694	82%

The personal and social harm that criminalising over 650,000 cannabis users in the last 28 years has done is virtually incalculable in terms of jobs lost, careers harmed, stigmatisation, relationships breaking up, as well as imprisonment and all its attendant horrors.

How many people have there been like Rosalind Henderson, a Scottish advocate's wife, who was sentenced to eight months in Corton Vale women's prison for growing 13 cannabis plants in her Perthshire home.[11] Or like Martin Dowell from Orkney who was sentenced to three months in prison for growing cannabis to ease his ME symptoms.[12] Or like Graeme Steel who was sentenced to nine months for growing cannabis plants at his home in the Borders because he didn't want to get his supply from criminal drug dealers?[13]

Here is just one indication of the financial cost to the tax payer that cannabis prohibition is responsible for:

In 1995, 7,086 people were sent to prison for all drug offences – and out of those 80 per cent of them were jailed for cannabis offences.[14] The average jail sentence for cannabis offenders was 21.1 months.[15] Given that it costs on average £26,700 per annum to keep someone in prison,[16] the overall cost to society for incarcerating cannabis offenders runs at over £266 million per year. And this is climbing every year.

There aren't enough prisons or courts to cope with this. The longer it goes on the more a whole generation of young people are being further alienated from the law and the police. This is a heavy and needless price for the rest of society to pay for the persecution of a harmless substance.

ARGUMENTS AGAINST THE LEGALISATION OF CANNABIS

It is worth considering the objections that Jack Straw, the British Home Secretary, raised when he tried to justify his position against decriminalising cannabis. He said that the effects of cannabis were not fully known, and that the drug could aggravate mental illness and lead to high rates of absenteeism. He argued specifically that:

> *"What I regard as so irresponsible about those who say we should decriminalise possession of small amounts of cannabis is: one thing which would follow, as night follows day, is that consumption would shoot up,"* adding, *"It would make law enforcement much more difficult and would be a betrayal of the futures of young people."* [17]

The old myth that cannabis is "a stepping stone" onto harder drugs is now so discredited that virtually no one who knows anything about the subject really uses it any more. The only credence this argument had in the first place is because cannabis smokers often have to buy their supplies from the same organisations who sell harder drugs like heroin. Mind you, after the disclosure that Jack Straw's brother Ed was an enthusiastic and regular user of cannabis in the sixties,[18] it is unlikely that we'll hear anymore "gateway drug" theories from

Mr Straw! His brother never slid down any imaginary "slippery slope" into heroin addiction, and by all accounts now holds down a responsible and well-paid job.

It is not inconceivable that dealers can manipulate the black market to create shortages of the less profitable drug like cannabis in order to create a larger market for a more profitable and addictive substance like heroin. There is enough evidence to show that this *does* happen, particularly with regards to the younger and impressionable buyers who are specifically targeted by these dealers.

Clearly, though, this is an overwhelming argument in favour of *separating* cannabis from the heroin dealers through legalising and licensing cannabis outlets where the sale of other drugs is forcibly excluded.

It would be wrong to say that cannabis use has no risks. All drugs carry some risk even if it is very small. Anyone suffering from mental illness such as schizophrenia should stay clear of any drug that hasn't been prescribed by a doctor. Heavy use of cannabis on a daily basis *can* lead to problems just as heavy use of alcohol does. Many heavy cannabis users are unemployed and their usage tends to be more a product of boredom than anything else. Tackling unemployment is the most effective method of combating any such problems with cannabis.

In Holland where drug use isn't treated as a criminal offence but a health and social issue there is an openness about *all* drug use which allows the caring professions to build an accurate picture of trends and problems. The number of people who use cannabis in Holland is estimated to be around 675,000 out of a population of 15 million.[19] Out of those, in 1993, 1,749 people were registered with Alcohol and Drugs Clinics because of problems associated with cannabis.[20] The Dutch authorities estimate that this is between 1 and 2 per cent of intensive cannabis users, that is to say those who use cannabis ten times or more a month, and 0.25 per cent of all cannabis smokers.[21] This is a very small percentage and almost insignificant in comparison to the problems associated with drugs like alcohol and tobacco.

The argument about the health risks associated with cannabis use will no doubt go on. Although there is a whole weight of reliable scientific and medical evidence which states that cannabis is a relatively safe drug to use, anti-drug campaigners continue to refuse to accept this. An editorial in *The Lancet*, one of the most respected medical journals in the world, stated that "smoking of cannabis, even long term, is not harmful to health."[22] Most people tend to respect the opinion of doctors rather than politicians when it comes down to health issues.

With the other arguments against legalising cannabis carrying about as much weight as a fistful of helium balloons, it is Jack Straw's claim that legalising cannabis would lead to "consumption shooting up" that needs answering.

In essence, Straw is saying that he will continue the criminalising of cannabis users *not* for what they are doing *now* but for what others *might* do in the future! And this is from the person in charge of the British legal system. Scary!

And what evidence does Jack Straw have for this claim? I would challenge Straw or anyone else who thinks along similar lines to come up with any concrete evidence to vindicate such a wild guess. The only place in the world where hard evidence and reliable data can be found on what would happen if cannabis was put on sale is Holland. It is also the only place in the world where some of the questions arising from the practicalities of licensing the sale of cannabis can be answered. A close look at the situation in Holland is necessary.

THE DUTCH EXPERIMENT

The Dutch government decided in 1975 that the use of cannabis was much less harmful than the criminalisation of users. Possession and sale of 30g and under was decriminalised. This came about partly through political pressure brought by groups such as the Dutch Provos – an organisation of cannabis activists who organised smoke-ins, demonstrations and other such stunts – as well as a realisation in official circles that it would benefit everyone if the cannabis market was separated from the black market in "hard drugs".[23]

At first youth clubs and then so-called "coffee shops" were given permission to sell cannabis so long as certain provisos were met. The premises were not allowed to have any other illegal drugs sold there. An age limit of 18 was to be strictly enforced. And most importantly, they were not allowed to advertise or promote the fact that cannabis was being sold inside. The maximum individual purchase (after a revision in 1995) is 5g per customer.

The first coffee shop legally selling cannabis – The Bulldog – opened in Amsterdam on 29th August 1978, and gradually they spread throughout Dutch cities and into some smaller towns. Amsterdam currently has over 400 coffee shops with around 1,200 open throughout the country.[24]

The outside of the coffee shops have no mention of cannabis. There are no pictures of plants or leafs. (One coffee shop in Rotterdam was dealt with for featuring a cannabis leaf on a promotional poster and forced to withdraw it.)

Inside, the coffee shops have two counters, one for the ordinary café – the sale of alcohol is not permitted in coffee shops although one or two flout this and are being targeted by the authorities – and one where a menu can be requested with a list of the various types of grass and solid hash on sale. The cannabis is high quality (from all around the world but mainly home-grown *Nederweit*) with few of the impurities of the "soap bar" Moroccan hash usually sold in the UK. The ambience too is usually mellow and friendly. A bit like a pub without the drunks. And they are open seven days a week.

The coffee shops act as a buffer for the people who want to smoke cannabis but don't want to come in contact with other drugs such as heroin. The biggest single charge laid against cannabis is that it leads on to harder drugs. While there is no evidence to back this up it can't be denied that when cannabis is in short supply unscrupulous dealers try and persuade their customers to take something else instead. (During the cannabis "drought" of 1996 in Scotland there was a marked increase in smoking heroin, and as if by "coincidence", a glut of cheap heroin suddenly appeared – with bags costing as little as £5.)

This type of problem has been banished by the Dutch coffee shop system. In 1995 the Dutch Ministry published a report *Drugs Policy In The Netherlands* which stated that as a consequence of an overall policy of harm reduction which included separating cannabis from the black market in heroin, heroin addiction had stabilised at a rate of 0.16 per cent of the population. Heroin addiction in countries like Britain and France had risen to 0.26 per cent of the population (in both cases) – 62 per cent higher. But more significantly, the average age of heroin addicts has steadily increased in Holland indicating that its use among younger people is falling. (It is also interesting to note that in the last twenty years there has been virtually no known abuse of solvents among young people.)

The report states: *"In some countries, total use (of drugs) has increased; in the Netherlands, drug consumption appears to have stabilised at the level it reached around 1980."*

From 1975, when cannabis was decriminalised, the use of cannabis actually *fell* for the first ten years,[25] an indisputable fact which completely and categorically refutes the unsubstantiated claims of

Jack Straw and friends. The Dutch authorities admit that cannabis use then increased from around the mid-eighties but this was largely in line with its rise in popularity in other European countries and is mainly attributable to the rise of acid house, the rave scene and other cultural factors including the drug culture that flourished alongside much of the music.

In Holland people are more relaxed about smoking cannabis, the glamour of its illegality has gone, and people know they can buy it whenever *they* want to, and not when dealers come hassling. These are the facts, Mr Straw. It is prohibition which leads to an increase in drug use rather than legalisation. Compare the Dutch example with here and you'll see that the continual steep rise in the UK figures for cannabis offences and cannabis seizures over the last thirty years confirm this.

The system in Holland *works*. It doesn't promote cannabis, it tolerates it. There is a difference. The Dutch have proven that they can successfully bring the sale of illegal drugs under control. If it works there it will work here. This is why the people who have made the effort to actually go out and examine the coffee shop system first-hand have come back recommending it.

The Lancet recommended the adoption of the Dutch policies in an editorial in 1996.[26] The chief medical officer of Copenhagen has recommended that his country should not only adopt the Dutch coffee shop system but also legalise state production and distribution of the sale of cannabis. The German state of Schleswig Holstein is considering adopting the Dutch model too.

If there is a problem with the Dutch system – and there is – it is that the production and distribution of cannabis is still in the hands of the black market. It isn't completely in the hands of the criminal underworld though, as many of the coffee shop suppliers are "legitimate" farmers of the crop and enthusiasts. The Dutch report states that one possible way of getting round this would be to license approximately 35,000 small-scale domestic growers of cannabis – and they suggest there are already more than that number in Holland – who would be able to meet demand.[27] That way there would be no need for supplies to be obtained from criminal sources. The report advocates cracking down harder on large-scale cultivation with a doubling of the maximum prison sentence to four years and heavier fines.[28]

However the gangster element is still there and acts much in the same anti-social way as it does in every other country. This has lead to a legal grey area which can only be eliminated by full legalisation and licensing of growers and vendors. The Dutch know this and would like to, but claim, like every other country, to be tied into the United Nations agreements which forbid the legalisation of illegal drugs in any member state.

When all the arguments of the cannabis prohibitionists in the UK fall flat on their faces it will be this last straw that they too will cling too. However, if the UK joins forces with the Dutch then neither country would be isolated on a policy of legalisation and the European-wide collapse of cannabis prohibition would soon follow, especially given the support that already exists for changing the drug laws in countries such as Switzerland, Denmark, Belgium and Germany. It just takes courage in standing up to the dictates of America who often use United Nations agreements as nothing more than a vehicle for an extension of their own domestic and foreign policies.

WHAT ABOUT OTHER DRUGS?

Cannabis is not the only psychoactive drug that is sold legally in Holland. A number of "smart shops" have opened up which work on a similar principle to the coffee shops but they sell magic mushrooms instead. These are sold in pots of tea, prepared food, or in pre-rolled joints which cost around £3 for a medium dose trip and about £4 for a strong dose trip. These "smart shops" distribute sensible harm reduction advice about how the drugs work, how long they last for, and how to make the trip as safe and enjoyable as possible. In fact, they are not that different from the shops run by the harm reduction organisations in Britain. Except that they sell the drugs on the premises. After getting medical advice which confirmed that these drugs didn't constitute a significant health risk the Dutch government decided to tolerate their sale.[29]

For drugs like ecstasy, amphetamines, LSD and cocaine this could be the best way forward, licensed *drug-specific* coffee shops which not only sell small amounts for personal use but dispense harm reduction advice on safer drug-taking as well as testing the purity and composition of the drugs themselves. This is important if people are no longer to be playing Russian roulette with unknown substances. The alternative, as always, is that people will simply buy their drugs on the black market with all the attendant risks to health and the enriching of criminals.

A lot more consultation and discussion will need to be done to get the actual mechanics of how these premises would work in practice but the principle is sound. Get these drugs out of the black market and all its attendant dangers and into an environment where any harm associated with the drugs can be reduced.

Commander John Grieve of the Metropolitan Police is one who agrees:

> "Licensing for illegal drugs including ecstasy should be explored, perhaps on the basis of licensed cafes in Amsterdam . . . Either we go to war with drug dealers across the globe, or we have to come up with new options." [30]

In a few years time, when measures like these have been adopted, and when overall drug use is falling as a result, and when people become more responsible about their drug use, and when the Treasury coffers are being filled with money to pay for the health service instead of it going to the criminal drug gangs, then we'll see politicians, the media and the general public all with only one baffling question about drugs on their lips: *Why the hell wasn't this done years ago?*

IT DOESN'T STOP HERE

This book doesn't really end here. Although it is as up-to-date as publishing schedules will allow, things are changing all the time. To continue to be relevant, this book may need to be updated and expanded to take into account new developments, feedback and any criticism. (The former will be closely monitored while the latter is always welcome.)

If you can think of any points that have been omitted, or need to be clarified or expanded, I'd like to know. Similarly, if you have any feedback, information, press cuttings, know of any books worth checking out, or hear of any events coming up, I can be contacted c/o Canongate Books, 14 High Street, Edinburgh, EH1. Or e-mail me direct at kevinw@canongate.co.uk where I'll also be developing a web-site with regular articles and updates on the drug debate.

The rest is down to continual lobbying, campaigning and arguing the case for change until the monolith cracks and then crumbles. Use your vote, your voice, and pen and paper, to make sure that MPs, local councillors, and newspaper editors know that the silent majority isn't prepared to stay silent any more.

Kevin Williamson, October 1997

REFERENCES AND SOURCES

AN INTRODUCTION

1.   The Scotsman, 9 Mar 1997, "CANNABIS LAW NEEDS REVIEW SAY LIB DEMS"

DRUG PROHIBITION: HOW IT CAME ABOUT

1.–5.   *The Forbidden Game*, Brian Inglis, 1975
6.   Scotland Against Drugs advertising campaign, 1996
7.   *Edinburgh Review*, Sydney Smith, 1830
8.   *The Forbidden Game*, Brian Inglis, 1975
9.   *ibid.*
10.   *The Face*, October 1993
11.   *The Sunday Times*, 15 July 1923
12.   *Prohibition Inside Out*, Roy Haynes, 1923
13.   *The Forbidden Game*, Brian Inglis, 1975
14.   *High Times Encyclopaedia Of Recreational Drugs*, 1978
15.   *The Face*, October 1993
16.   *High Times Encyclopaedia Of Recreational Drugs*, 1978
17.   *The Forbidden Game*, Brian Inglis, 1975
18.   *ibid.*
19.   *Home Office Statistical Bulletins.*
20.   *ibid.*
21.   *The Forbidden Game*, Brian Inglis, 1975
22.–26.   *The Emperor Wears No Clothes*, Jack Herer, 1994

THE WAR AGAINST DRUGS HAS BEEN LOST: IT'S OFFICIAL

1.   *The Scotsman*, 28 Aug 1997, "US AND MEXICO IN NEW DRUG WAR STRATEGY"

2. *The Guardian*, 27 June 1997, "DRUGS '8pc OF WORLD TRADE'"

3. *The Scotsman*, 28 Aug 1997, "SECRET SERVICES TO DECLARE WAR ON ASIA DRUG BARONS"

4. *Daily Mirror*, 29 Aug 1997, "No 1 TARGET IS £2bn-A-YEAR HEROIN BOSS"

5. *Independent on Sunday*, 28 Sep 1997, "THE DETECTIVE'S VIEW"

6. *The Scotsman*, 28 Aug 1997, "US AND MEXICO IN NEW DRUG WAR STRATEGY"

7. *The Guardian*, 24 Feb 1997, "GOVERNOR 'AIDS MEXICAN DRUG TRADE'"

8. *The Scotsman*, 28 Aug 1997, "US AND MEXICO IN NEW DRUG WAR STRATEGY"

9. *ibid.*

10. *The Scotsman*, 12 Feb 1997, "VIETNAM'S REVOLUTION GOES UP IN SMOKE"

11. *The Politics of Heroin*, Alfred W. McCoy, 1972

12. *The Herald*, 19 Oct 1996, "ESTATE THAT IS ALSO A BATTLE-GROUND"

13. *The Scotsman*, 28 Aug 1997, "POLICE IGNORED FCB REPORT"

14. *The Scotsman*, 28 Aug 1997, "PAISLEY GANGSTERS USED FEAR OF DEATH IN £320,000 FCB FRAUD"

15. *ibid.*

16. *The Scotsman*, 18 Mar, 1997, "RECORD £500m IN DRUGS SEIZED"

17. *ibid.*

18.–22. *Home Office Statistical Bulletins*

23. *The Scotsman*, 18 Mar, 1997, "RECORD £500m IN DRUGS SEIZED"

24. *The Scotsman*, 20 Aug 1997, "80% OF PRISONERS 'ADDICTED TO DRUGS'"

25. *The Scotsman*, 30 Sep 1996, "NINE OUT OF TEN INMATES ON DRUGS"

26. *Daily Record*, 19 May 1977, "BLAIR'S CRUSADE ON JUNKIE CROOKS"

27. *The Guardian*, 25 Aug 1997, EDITORIAL

28. *Scotland on Sunday*, 7 Jan 1996, "GLASGOW ADDICTS COST

500m A YEAR"

29.   *Daily Record*, 19 May 1997, "BLAIR'S CRUSADE ON JUNKIE CROOKS"

30.   *U.S. Government Prison Statistics*

31.   *The Herald*, 9 Jan 1996, "IGNORANCE IS A GREATER ENEMY OF SOCIETY THAN DRUG-PUSHERS"

32.   *Daily Record*, 1 July 1997, "PROFIT CHEER FOR BREWERS"

SCOTLAND AGAINST DRUGS?

1.   *The Scotsman*, 3 May 1996, "DRUGS CAMPAIGN 'WILL NOT PREACH'"

2.   *The Scotsman*, 10 July 1996, "ANTI-DRUG DRIVE WILL HIT THE STREETS"

3.   *Big Issue Scotland*, 13 Feb 1997, "SHOCK HORROR OR JUST SHOCKING"

4.   Taped interview with K. Williamson, 21 May 1997

5.   *The Scotsman*, 21 June 1997, "ECSTASY DEATH FUELS DRUGS ROW"

6.   *Scotland on Sunday*, 7 Jan 1996, "DRUGS – THE CALL TO ARMS WAITS ON TACTICS"

7.   *ibid*.

8.   *The Guardian*, 30 May 1996, "MPS ATTACKED OVER DRUGS HYPOCRICY"

9.   *The Scotsman*, 8 May 1996, "A JOURNEY FROM RAZZMATAZZ TO REALITY"

10.   *The Scotsman*, 3 May 1996, "DRUGS CAMPAIGN 'WILL NOT PREACH'"

11.   *The Guardian*, 17 Sep 1996, "WHEN LIFE IS JUST BURNED AWAY"

12.   Taped interview with K. Williamson, 21 May 1997

13.   *The Scotsman*, 10 July 1996, "ANTI-DRUG DRIVE WILL HIT THE STREETS"

14.   *Edinburgh Evening News*, 4 Sep 1996, "LET'S JUST SAY IT'S NOT GOOD ENOUGH"

15.   *The Scotsman*, 8 Oct 1996, "DRUGS CAMPAIGN TARGETS IMAGE-CONCIOUS TEENAGERS"

16.   *The Scotsman*, 4 Nov 1996, "FORSYTH TO BACK SHOCK ANTI-DRUG CAMPAIGN"

17.   *The Scotsman*, 6 Dec 1996, "HARD HITTING ADS PLAY ON DRUG FEARS"

18.   *Daily Record*, 23 June 1997, "JUST SAY NO"

19.   *Big Issue Scotland*, 13 Feb 1997, "SHOCK HORROR OR JUST SHOCKING"

20.   *ibid.*

21.   *The Scotsman*, 21 June 1997

22.   *Scotland on Sunday*, 6 July 1997, "THE SAD TRUTH ABOUT SCOTLAND AGAINST DRUGS"

23.   *Scotland on Sunday*, 13 July 1997, "DRUG EXPERTS ATTACK SAD'S CRUSADE"

24.   *Scotland on Sunday*, 22 June 1997, "SURVEY FINDS 32% OF SCOTS ADULTS HAVE TAKEN DRUGS"

A NEW APPROACH BASED ON HARM REDUCTION

1.   *Independent on Sunday*, 28 Jan 1996, "GENERATION WHY NOT?"

2.   *Scotland on Sunday*, 22 June 1997, "FEAR, CONFUSION AND IGNORANCE"

3.   *Scotland Against Drugs* advertising campaign, 1997

4.   *Crew 2000 Survey*, Feb 1996, "TRENDS & RECOMMENDATIONS O YOUNG PEOPLE'S DRUG USE IN GLASGOW"

5.   *Crew 2000 Survey*, Feb 1994, "ADOLESCENT DRUG USE IN EDINBURGH"

6.   *ibid.*

7.   *The Scotsman*, 21 June 1997

8.   *ibid.*

9.   *Scotland on Sunday*, 6 July 1997, "THE SAD TRUTH ABOUT SCOTLAND AGAINST DRUGS"

10.   *Scotland on Sunday*, 22 June 1997, "FEAR, CONFUSION AND IGNORANCE"

11.   *Crew 2000 Survey*, Feb 1994, "ADOLESCENT DRUG USE IN EDINBURGH"

12.   *The Scotsman*, 26 Mar 1997, "BLAIR REJECTS KIRK'S SOFT LINE ON DRUGS"

13.   *Daily Mirror*, 29 Aug 1997
14.   *Mr Nice*, Howard Marks
15.   *Microsoft Network News*, July 97, "POLICE CHIEF WARNS OF MASSIVE INCREASE IN DRUG ABUSE"

THE CASE FOR THE DECRIMINALISATION OF DRUG USE

1.   *Daily Record*, 26 March 1997, "FIGHT THIS DRUGS EVIL"
2.   *The Scotsman*, 26 Mar 1997, "BLAIR REJECTS KIRK'S SOFT LINE ON DRUGS"
3.   *Essay On Liberty*, John Stuart Mill, 1859
4.–8.   Government Statistics taken from *Ecstasy & The Dance Culture*, Nicholas Saunders
9.   *The Scotsman*, 18 May 1995, "MYSTERIOUS AND MAGICAL BUT K2 IS ALSO A KILLER"
10.   *The Herald*, 9 Jan 1996, "IGNORANCE IS A GREATER ENEMY OF SOCIETY THAN DRUG-PUSHERS"
11.   *Crew 2000 Survey*, Feb 1994, "ADOLESCENT DRUG USE IN EDINBURGH"
12.   *Scotland on Sunday*, 22 June 1997, "FEAR, CONFUSION AND IGNORANCE"

WHICH DRUGS SHOULD BE TAKEN OUT OF THE BLACK MARKET?

1.   *Home Office Statistical Bulletins*
2.   *ibid.*
3.   *ibid.*

HEROIN – A SPECIAL CASE, A PRIORITY CASE

1.   *The Odyssey*, Homer
2.   *The Forbidden Game*, Brian Inglis, 1975
3.   *Home Office Statistical Bulletins*
4.   *ibid.*
5.   *The Big Issue*, 18 Dec 1995 "SMACK IS BACK"
6.   ibid.
7.–10. *Druglink* May/June 1996, "HEROIN IN THE 1990's"

11. *The Scotsman*, 9 Dec 1996, "FACING DOWN SMACK"

12. *Scotland on Sunday*, 7 Jan 1996, "GLASGOW ADDICTS COST 500m A YEAR"

13. *World Health Organisation Study*, 1994

14. *ibid.*

15. *Scotland on Sunday*, 7 Jan 1996, "GLASGOW ADDICTS COST 500m A YEAR"

16. *ibid.*

17. *ibid.*

18. *Daily Record*, 19 May 1957, "BLAIR'S CRUSADE AGAINST JUNKIE CROOKS"

19. *Home Office Statistics*

20. *The Sunday Times*, 5 May, "THE GREAT STATE FIX"

21. *Lothian & Borders Police*

22. *Scotland on Sunday*, 7 Jan 1996, "GLASGOW ADDICTS COST 500m A YEAR"

23. *ibid.*

24. *ibid.*

25. *The Scotsman*, 20 Aug 1997, "ADDICTS PLOICY CUTS DRUG DEATHS"

26. *The Sunday Times*, 5 May, "THE GREAT STATE FIX"

27. *ibid.*

28. *The Scotsman*, 4 May 1997, Letter from CJ Spry, Greater Glasgow Drug Action Team

29. *The Big Issue Scotland*, 19 Jan 1996, "DEADLY DRUG SECRET EXPOSED"

30. *Home Office Statistical Bulletins*

31. *ibid.*

32. *ibid.*

33. *Scotland on Sunday*, 27 April 1997, "HEROIN CURE KILLS ADDICTS"

34. *Royal Society of Medicine*, Report, 1994

35. *The Sunday Times*, 5 May, "THE GREAT STATE FIX"

36. *Drug Policy In The 90's Conference*, paper presented by Anthony Henman, "HARM REDUCTION ON MERSEYSIDE, 1985-1995"

37. *British Journal of Hospital Medicine*, Vol 52, No 213, 1994, "DRUG MISUSE AND SOCIAL COST"

38. *Liverpool Echo*, 4 Feb 1991, "STORE GIANT BACKS THE WAR ON DRUGS"

39.–42. *The Scotsman*, 26 Sep 1997, "SWISS TO VOTE ON ENDING STATE HEROIN HAND OUTS FOR ADDICTS"

43. *The Times*, 22 June 1967, "GROWING BLACK MARKET" (Letters Page)

44. *Home Office Statistical Bulletins*

45. *ibid*

46. *Scotland on Sunday*, 7 Jan 1996, "GLASGOW ADDICTS COST 500m A YEAR"

LICENSING THE SALE OF CANNABIS

1. *The Face*, October 1993

2. *The Scotsman*, 3 July 1997, "DOCTOR'S PLEA TO MAKE CANNABIS MEDICINES LEGAL"

3. *The Forbidden Game*, Brian Inglis, 1975

4. *The Scotsman*, 9 Mar 1997, "CANNABIS LAW NEEDS REVIEW SAY LIB DEMS"

5. *The Guardian*, 29 Sep 1997, "ONE IN THREE SMOKE POT BY 14"

6. *Scotland on Sunday*, 22 June 1997, "FEAR, CONFUSION AND IGNORANCE"

7. *The Scotsman*, 21 Nov 1996, "SURVEY FINDS LIBERAL ATTITUDE TO SOFT DRUGS"

8. *The Times*, 24 July 1967

9. *Home Office Statistical Bulletins*

10. *ibid.*

11. UKCIA Website 1996, http://www.foobar.co.uk/users/ukcia

12. *The Herald*, 21 Feb 1996, "DRUGS SENTENCE IS CUT IN HALF"

13. *The Scotsman*, 26 Mar 1997, "JAIL DID NOT ALTER VIWS OF DAVID STEEL'S SON"

14. *Home Office Statistical Bulletins*

15. *ibid.*

16. *Annual Report*, HM Inspector Of Prisons, 1996

17. *The Guardian*, 29 Sep 1997, "ONE IN THREE SMOKE POT BY 14"

18. *Independent on Sunday*, 5 Oct 1997, "DRUG FIGURES SHOW WHY LAW MUST CHANGE"

19. *Dutch Ministry of Health* report, 1995, "DRUG POLICY IN THE NETHERLANDS"

20. *ibid*.

21. *ibid*.

22. *The Lancet*, 11 Nov 1995, Editorial, "DEGLAMORISING CANNABIS"

23. *Dutch Ministry of Health* report, 1995, "DRUG POLICY IN THE NETHERLANDS"

24. *ibid*.

25. *ibid*

26. *The Lancet*, 1995, Editorial

27. *Dutch Ministry of Health* report, 1995, "DRUG POLICY IN THE NETHERLANDS"

28. *ibid*.

29. *ibid*.

30. *Ecstasy Reconsidered*, Nicholas Saunders, 1997

FURTHER READING

A (short) bibliography of books I've found useful in shedding light on a complex subject:

Albert, R., Leary, T. & Metzner, R. (1990) *The Psychedelic Experience*, Citadel Press.

Algren, N. (1998) *The Man With The Golden Arm*, Rebel Inc.

Burroughs, W.S. (1953, 1977) *Junky*, Penguin Books.

Casteneda, C. (1970) *The Teachings of Don Juan*, Penguin

Cooper Jr, C. (1960, 1996) *The Scene*, Payback Press.

Collin, M. (1997) *Altered State: The Story of Ecstasy Culture and Acid House*, Serpent's Tail.

De Quincy, T. (1821, 1994) *Confessions Of An English Opium Eater*, Wordsworth.

Haining, P. (ed) (1974) *The Hashish Club*, Peter Owen.

Herer, J. (1990, 1995) *The Emperor Wears No Clothes: Hemp & The Marijuana Conspiracy*, HEMP/Green Planet Company

High Times magazine, (1978)*The High Times Encyclopaedia Of Recreational Drugs*, Stonehill.

Huxley, A. (1951, 1961) *The Doors of Perception*, Penguin Books

Inglis, B. (1975,1977) *The Forbidden Game, A Social History Of Drugs*, Coronet.

Leary, T. (1965, 1970) *The Politics Of Ecstasy*, Paladin

Margolis, J. (1978) *Jack Margolis' Complete Book of Recreational Drug*, Price/Stern/Sloan.

Marks, H. (1997) *Mr Nice*, Minerva,

McCoy, A.W. (1972, 1991) *The Politics of Heroin*, Lawrence Hill Books

Miller, J & Koral, R. (eds.) (1995) *The White Rabbit, A Psychedelic Reader*, Chronicle Books.

Rosenthal, E. *Marijuana Question? Ask Ed*

Sabbag, R (1976, 1998) *Snowblind*, Rebel Inc.

Saunders, N (1995) *Ecstasy and the Dance Culture*, Nicholas Saunders.

Saunders, N. (1997) *Ecstasy Reconsidered*, Nicholas Saunders.

Shulgin, A. (1991) *PIKHAL, (Phenethylamines I Have Known And Loved)*, Transform Press

Stevens, J. (1987, 1993) *Storming Heaven, LSD and the American Dream*, Flamingo.

Stewart, T. (1987) *The Heroin Users*, Pandora.

Strausbaugh, J and Donald Blaise, D. (eds.) (1991) *The Drug User*, Blast Books, Inc.

Trocchi, A.(1961, 1966) *Cain's Book*, Jupiter Books.

Welsh, I. (1993) *Trainspotting*, Secker & Warburg.

Young, J. (1971) *The Drugtakers*, Paladin

ACKNOWLEDGEMENTS

Since I started working on this book, I've been fortunate enough to have received plenty of encouragement, help, information and ideas from all sorts of people. Useful press cuttings have mysteriously appeared in my letterbox, anonymous e-mails arrive with advice and info, and books have been donated or loaned (and you'll all get them back, don't worry!). Others who I have approached for information have been incredibly helpful and enthusiastic. A special thanks has to go to Stu Young, Liz Skelton, Willie McBride, Lorti, Dr John Marks, and everyone at Crew 2000, Enhance, Scottish Drugs Forum, and Turning Point whose help one way or another was/is immeasurable. Keep up the invaluable work you're doing. More thanks to Petey and Nagina for doing what you do best, to Paul and Irvine for opening certain doors, to Rosie, Angeline, Claire, Graeme S, Innes Reekie, Will Lawson and Roger Lewis for books, ideas and inspiration of sorts, to Colin for the final reading, and to Fiona for the loan of the computer. And to the countless others who have helped enlighten me on the subject, cheers.

Biggest thanks and most respect to Charlotte, Jamie, and everyone at Canongate for keeping the faith when deadlines merged into lost weekends and things seemed to be going a bit *askew*.

And finally, this book is dedicated to my daughter Marie. Hopefully, by the time you leave school, this country and others will have a more progressive and enlightened approach to drug use and people will look back on the disastrous twentieth century experiment in drug prohibition with a mixture of horror and disbelief.

REBEL inc.

Taking over where the underground literary magazine left off - Rebel inc, the book imprint, has successfully published challenging, but accessible texts aimed at extending the domain of counter culture literature.

Children of Albion Rovers - editor Kevin Williamson
Best-selling collection of novellas from Irvine Welsh, Alan Warner, Gordon Legge, James Meek, Laura Hird, and Paul Reekie.
"It is billed as a "frenetic breakbeat of Scottish social surrealism and urban mythology" but is better than that."
Literary Review
"A fistful of Caledonian classics" Loaded
£5.99pbk - isbn 0 86241 731 7

Nail - Laura Hird
Collection of short stories that delves deep into the power struggle between the sexes and generations.
"Roars like a lion on the printed page" ID magazine
"a dazzling new writer" The Bookseller
£8.99pbk - isbn 0 86241 677 9

Hunger - Knut Hamsun
A new translation by Sverre Lyngstad
with an introduction by Duncan Mclean
"Hunger is the crux of Hamsun's claims to mastery. This is the classic novel of humiliation, even beyond Dostoevsky."
The Observer
£6.99pbk - isbn 0 86241 625 6

Helen and Desire - Alexander Trocchi
Introduction by Edwin Morgan
"…a spicily pornographic tale…Trocchi has a keen eye for the absurdities of the genre." The Scotsman
£6.99pbk - isbn 0 86241 629 9

Fup - Jim Dodge

Illustrated by Harry Horse

"A stupendous little book that will knock your socks off...It is also hilariously funny. Fup makes me yearn to pull out all the over-worked cliches of a thirsty critic: it is a jewel, a gem, a diamond in the cesspool of life" San Francisco Chronicle

£7.99hbk - isbn 0 86241 734 1

Kill Kill Faster Faster - Joel Rose

"...disturbingly compulsive, intensely erotic and darkly entertaining...Streetwise, stylish, gutsy and utterly compelling." Books Magazine

"...set to become a cult classic" Publishing News

£6.99pbk - isbn 0 86241 697 3

Revenge of the Lawn - Richard Brautigan

Introduction by Gordon Legge

"He has such a lovely touch: a born writer...he can't be dull" The Sunday Times

Brautigan in miniature, with 62 ultra-short stories.

£6.99pbk - isbn 0 86241 723 6

The Blind Owl - Sadegh Hedayat

Introduction by Alan Warner

"One of the most extraordinary books I've ever read. Chilling and beautiful." The Guardian

"An extraordinary work" Times Literary Supplement

£6.99pbk - isbn 0 86241 676 0

This is only a selection of Rebel inc. titles. If you wish further information, please do not hesitate to contact us at the address below. Titles are available from all good book shops or can be ordered directly from:

Canongate Books, 14 High Street, Edinburgh, EH1 1TE
Tel. 0131 557 5111 Fax 0131 557 5211 email info@canongate.co.uk
website http://www.canongate.co.uk

All forms of payment are accepted and p&p is free to any address in the U.K. Please specify if you want to join the Rebel inc. mailing list.